NORTHUMBERLAND

TOWNS & VILLAGES

Lydia Speakman

Series Editor: Terry Marsh

SIGMA Leisure

Published by Sigma Leisure – an imprint of
Sigma Press, 1 South Oak Lane, Wilmslow, Cheshire SK9 6AR, England.

British Library Cataloguing in Publication Data
A CIP record for this book is available from the British Library.

ISBN: 1-85058-639-X

Series Editor: Terry Marsh

Typesetting and Design by: Sigma Press, Wilmslow, Cheshire.

Cover Design: MFP Design & Print

Cover photographs: main picture – the harbour at Craster; smaller pictures, from top – Elsdon church; Blanchland village; Dunstanburgh castle

Photographs: by the author

Map: Morag Perrott

Printed by: MFP Design & Print

Dedication

For Meryn, my Northumbrian girl – born during the research and writing of this book.

Contents

Introduction 1

Explanatory Notes 1

Tourist Information Centres 3

Northumberland on the Internet 3

Northumberland 4

The Formation of a Landscape 4

Prehistory 6

The Romans and Hadrian's Wall 7

Early Christianity – the Golden Age of Northumbria 8

The Normans 9

The Border Troubles 11

A Civilised Landscape 12

Lead Mining 13

Coal Mining and the Railways 14

Northumberland Today 14

The Towns and Villages 15

Index 107

NORTHUMBRIA

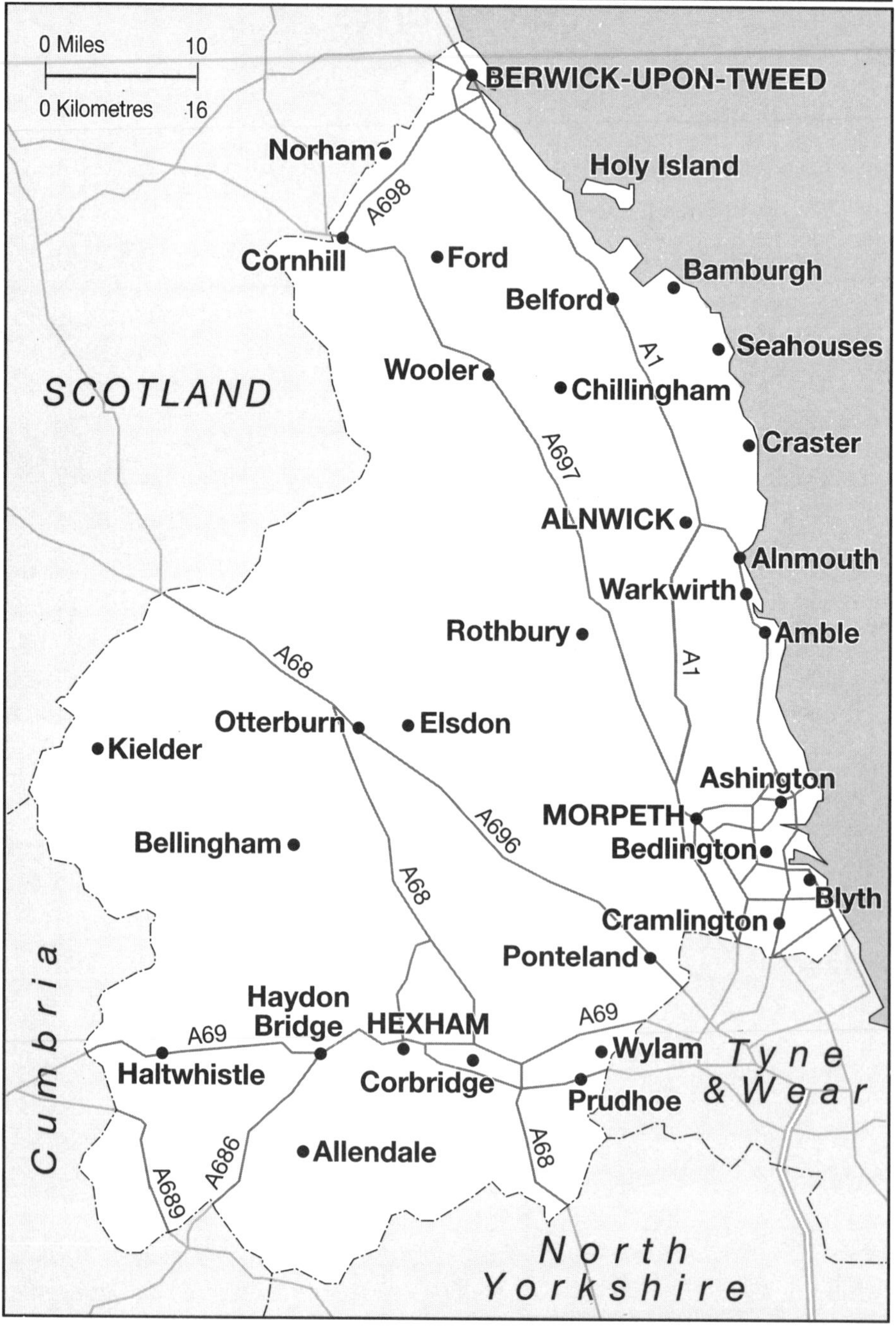

0 Miles 10
0 Kilometres 16
BERWICK-UPON-TWEED
Norham
Holy Island
A698
Cornhill
Ford
Bamburgh
Belford
Seahouses
A1
Wooler
Chillingham
SCOTLAND
Craster
A697
ALNWICK
Alnmouth
Warkwirth
Rothbury
Amble
A1
A68
Otterburn
Elsdon
Kielder
Ashington
MORPETH
A696
Bedlington
Bellingham
A68
Blyth
Cramlington
Ponteland
Cumbria
Haydon Bridge
HEXHAM
A69
A69
Wylam
Haltwhistle
Corbridge
Prudhoe
Tyne & Wear
A686
A68
Allendale
A689
North Yorkshire

Introduction

The 'Towns and Villages of Britain' is a series of titles detailing a county-by-county approach to the many delights and fascinations of our country's cities, towns, villages and hamlets. There is much of interest and value throughout our towns and villages, but not all of it is widely documented, and some of it, particularly local customs, folklore and traditions, is in danger of being lost forever. By bringing all this information together, county-by-county, it becomes possible to build a unique and substantially comprehensive library of knowledge.

All of the books in the series are compiled to the same specification and in gazetteer format, and include information about the way or the reason a town or village evolved; references to anything associated with the preservation of the past, such as museums, heritage centres, historic or prehistoric sites, battle sites, places of worship and other locally or architecturally important buildings. Landscape features are also detailed, including important natural history sites, geological sites, water features, etc. as is information about important local people, and details of events or traditions, such as well-dressings and rush-bearing ceremonies. There are also notes about any significant present-day informal amenity/recreational features, like country parks, open access land, Areas of Outstanding Natural Beauty, nature reserves, and Sites of Special Scientific Interest. Finally, information is given on any significant Roman or prehistory context, and any anecdotal or endemic folklore references associated with the town or village which might illustrate a particular way of life or social development. The books are therefore eminently suitable for anyone interested in their own locality or in local history; students of history, folklore and related subjects; professional journalists wanting up-to-date and comprehensive information; public relations and similar businesses; photographers and artists, and, of course, tourists and visitors to the counties.

Explanatory Notes

It has been suggested that to qualify as a village, a 'community' must possess a school, a pub, a post office and a church. Such a requirement, however, excludes a large number of places that are of immense interest, many having important historical associations, and which have played a vital part in the development of the county and its people. So, for the purposes of the books in this series, the criteria for inclusion have been kept deliberately simple: there must be something of interest about the place; or it must have associations with events and people of countywide or wider significance.

Often, the 'something of interest' will simply be the village church (its history, contents or architecture), or its green or a river bridge. In addition, the village may be important to the heritage of the county because it maintains the traditions, ways and beliefs of local culture, or has played a key role in the social, economic or political history of the county or the country as a whole. Only occasionally, however, is the village pub of special interest in this context, and often the development of large supermarkets within easy travelling distance of the villages has, sadly, signalled the demise of the traditional village shop. Local schools have often been swallowed up by larger schools, and far too many post offices are proving difficult to sustain as viable concerns. So, while that 'classic' definition of a village has much to commend it, in reality it is today too restrictive.

Quite what makes a town is another, arguable, matter. But the precise definition is not too important here; it's the place and its people, not its status, that matters. As a very broad distinction, that no-one should take seriously, a 'hamlet' (a few of which appear in these books) is a distinct community, while a 'village' could be said to be a hamlet with a church, and a 'town' is a village with a market.

In many cases, the historical development of the community, whether a tiny village, a town or a city, is fascinating in itself, and so it is that each entry gradually builds up a picture of the county that is unique. That is what this book endeavours to portray, in a logical and easily accessible way, as well as being a source of reference.

Inevitably, there will be places that have been omitted that others might argue should have been included. But the value each community has to bring to a work of this nature has been carefully weighed; invariably, borderline cases have been given the benefit of the doubt and included.

It is equally clear that, taken to its logical conclusion, this book would be ten times larger, and there has had to be a considerable degree of selective editing to make it of manageable size. One day, perhaps, there could be one book that says everything there is to say about the county, but could we afford to buy it? Could we carry it? Would we want it, when part of the beauty of what does exist is the range of voices and shades of opinion so many different authors can bring?

Following the General Introduction, the book becomes a gazetteer, listing the towns and villages of the county in alphabetical order.

After each town or village name there appears, in square brackets, [ ], the name of the relevant district council (see below).

Next appears a two-letter, four-figure grid reference, which will pinpoint the settlement to within half a mile (one kilometre). This is followed by an approximate distance from some other, usually larger, settlement, together with an equally approximate direction indicator.

Those features or people 'of interest' directly associated with the settlement are highlighted in bold text, while an index lists other features or people only incidentally associated.

Where information is given about events, such as agricultural shows, or facilities, such as museums, details of dates and hours of opening are usually available from any of the Tourist Information Centres listed below.

Tourist Information Centres

Thre are four main TICs in Northumberland – all of which are open all year:

ALNWICK (including Rothbury, Amble, Warkworth and Craster):
The Shambles, Alnwick,
Northumberland, NE66 1TN
Tel: 01665 510665
Fax: 01665 510447
E-Mail: mmanion@alnwick.gov.uk

BERWICK-UPON-TWEED (including Seahouses, Bamburgh, Holy Island and Wooler):
106 Marygate, Berwick-upon-Tweed,
TD15 1DT
Tel: 01289 330733
Fax: 01269 330448
E-Mail:
1s@berwick-upon-tweed.gov.uk

HEXHAM (including Hadrian's Wall, Kielder, Prudhoe, Haltwhistle and North Pennines):
The Manor Office, Hallgate, Hexham,
NE46 1XD
Tel: 01434 605225
Fax: 01434 600325
E-Mail:
tourism section@tynedale.gov.uk

MORPETH (including Ponteland, Druridge Bay and South East Northumberland): The Chantry,
Bridge Street, Morpeth, NE61 1PJ
Tel: 01670 511323
Fax: 01670 511326
E-Mail:
webmaster@castlemorpeth.co.uk

Northumberland on the Internet

In addition to the e-mail addresses listed above, there is an excellent official web site with many links to other sites:
www.northumberland.gov.uk

Northumberland

The most striking feature about Northumberland is its sheer emptiness. Much of the county is covered by huge tracts of uninhabited moorland stretching far into the horizon. Northumberland's past has shaped the settlement patterns and character of its towns and villages, just as much as its unforgiving terrain. This is borderland country, once the edge of the Roman Empire and the focus of centuries of Anglo-Scottish conflict. Throughout the Border Wars, Northumberland was a buffer zone between two hostile kingdoms and the accompanying skirmishes and lawlessness left much of the area as empty wasteland. This has ensured the survival of a wealth of archaeological remains from prehistoric times to the Dark Ages and beyond, together with a unique architectural heritage of defensive buildings and fortifications.

Writing in the early 18th century, Daniel Defoe described Northumberland as, "a long coasting county . . . bounded by the mountains of Stainmore and Cheviot on the west, which are in some places inaccessible, in many unpassable. Here is abundant business for the antiquary: every place shews you ruined castles, Roman altars, inscriptions, monuments of battles, of heroes killed and armies routed."

The great historic Northumbrian landmarks of Hadrian's Wall, Lindisfarne Priory and the medieval coastal castles form only a small part of this heritage. It is in the towns and villages with the remains of crumbling pele towers, ancient churches and prehistoric standing stones that the dramatic story of Northumberland and its people can be fully appreciated. This book is designed to introduce you to the history of Northumberland and provide a guide to its towns and villages, their surroundings and their buildings, but above all the stories of the communities that built them.

The Formation of a Landscape

Northumberland is a relatively new county created in 1844 when the lands of North Durham (Norhamshire, Islandshire and Bedlingtonshire) were incorporated into an administrative county. Today it no longer includes the city of Newcastle, but extends from the River Tyne and the foothills of the North Pennines in the south to the Cheviots and River Tweed in the north. In between is a magnificent coastline of almost empty sandy beaches and craggy headlands, and further west lush green farmland and wooded river valleys leading to the wild open moorland of the Cheviot Hills. Underlying these landscapes are rocks dating back over 400 million years, which influenced the way this land was first settled and farmed.

The great volcanoes which formed the Cheviot Hills left behind volcanic lavas of pinkish rock called andesite which overlays much of the central granite core. These high, round fells rising to a height of 2673ft (815m) are now covered in a sea of coarse grassland and peat hags. But millions of years ago the Cheviot massif was an island in a shallow sea. The sands from this former seabed became easily eroded shales and sandstone known as the Cementstone Group which are found in the broad, low-lying vales of the Coquet, Aln, Breamish and Till rivers. Today these valleys are a landscape of farms, hedges and green fields and were some of the first in Northumberland to be colonised by early Man.

A broad arc of fell sandstone, which forms a series of high crags and scarp slopes facing the Cheviots, was formed by subsequent deposits of sand from a once great river. This great angular ridge extends from the Kyloe hills, Simonside Hills, the Harbottle Hills and the Larriston Fells on the Cumbrian border. Covered in heather and bracken, with poor sandy soils, these fells have mostly been given over to sheep and grouse or covered in conifer plantation. The sandstone is good building material and since Roman times has been used in cottages, castles and churches throughout Northumberland.

The south-west of the county is dominated by later sedimentary rocks laid down in the carboniferous period. They consist of alternating layers of sandstone, shales, limestone and coal and are known as the Scremerston series. In places it is overlaid by limestone. It has created a typical Pennine landscape of heather-clad sandstone hills with the occasional rugged outcrop such as Ottercops and the Wannies, interspersed with areas of green fields divided by soft grey limestone walls. Here the valleys are much narrower and more isolated – which in the case of the North Tyne and the Rede valleys was to encourage the development of a very wild and distinctive border society. Large areas of this part of Northumberland are now covered in modern forest plantations, including the Wark and Kielder Forests. Further south, in the North Pennines Area of Outstanding Natural Beauty (AONB), hill farming still dominates among the ruins of deserted lead mines.

The Northumberland lowlands stretch in a crescent around these moors and hills, from the River Tweed in the north down to Tynemouth and along the River Tyne. Here heavy boulder clays overlay the solid rock, creating a fertile coastal plain that has been farmed since prehistoric times. Here are a scattering of attractive hamlets, villages and country estates set among a countryside of hedges and small pockets of woodland. In the south-east thick seams of coal were found and these stimulated the growth and development of a mighty industrial heartland built on coal, the railways and shipbuilding.

Perhaps one of the most dramatic natural landscape features in Northumberland is Great Whin Sill. This immense rocky outcrop begins at the Farne islands and continues down the coast, crowned on the way by the castles of Lindisfarne, Bamburgh and Dunstanburgh, before heading inland, where it forms the central section of Hadrian's Wall, before ending in the Durham Dales at High Force. It was created around 295 million years ago during a period dominated by the Armorican earthquakes which tilted and shaped the Northumberland landscape. During this process molten rock from the earth's core, magma, was forced upwards to the surface, creating a hard, dark grey rock, quartz dolerite, known as whinstone which has formed a series of magnificent escarpments.

Prehistory

From the very earliest times man has left his mark on the Northumberland landscape: clearing forests, rearing stocks and cultivating the land. It is a process which began with the gradual improvements in the climate after the end of the last Ice Age. Around 8000BC, relatively small groups of Mesolithic people migrated into northern England and southern Scotland. Flints and cherts from this period have been found in mid-Tynedale and Allendale. These early people were largely nomadic, depending on hunting and gathering food.

During the fifth millennium BC, Neolithic settlers began to arrive in northern Britain and began to grow crops and keep sheep and goats. Trees and scrubland were cleared in the lowland and valleys around Coquetdale, lower Breamish and upper Till valleys, where the characteristic polished axes of the Neolithic period have been found. By the last few centuries of the third millennium BC, it appears that a highly organised, late Neolithic social structure had evolved, with complex religious and burial rites which saw the construction of long stone cairns such as those around Redesdale (Bellshiel Law) and on Dod Hill.

The Beaker Folk migrated into Northumberland from the Rhineland and the Low Countries, bringing with them a knowledge of how to work copper and bronze. They were so named after their burial sites, which often contain a characteristic beaker lying within a stone cist. Northumberland contains a wealth of Bronze Age burial sites dating from around 2000BC, as well remains of standing stones and stone circles. Many of these stone monoliths are covered in elaborate cup and ring markings, in which a hollow is surrounded by a series of concentric rings. Some of the best examples can be found on Lordenshaws, and Weet Moor. Evidence of Bronze Age settlements consisting of small groups of unenclosed huts and simple field systems have been found around the lower slopes of the Cheviot Hills.

Around 1000BC it appears that the climate in Britain became much cooler and wetter. At the same time there was an influx of new settlers, the Celts, who introduced the use of iron and new settlement patterns based around hill forts. No one fully understands the role and purpose of the hill forts built in this period or the sudden need for new defensive structures. However, the conical shape of many of Northumberland's hills seems to lend themselves to simple fort construction. Excavations of these sites have revealed that often they contained between fifteen and twenty timber houses enclosed within timber stockades covering about an acre (0.4ha). Later, earthen and stone ramparts replaced these timber palisades, often with extensive ditches. Many of Northumberland's Iron Age hill forts have been overlaid with later Romano-British huts, whose stone circles are often visible within the ramparts. There are over one hundred and fifty hill forts in Northumberland, some of the most spectacular can be found in the Breamish valley and upper Coquetdale.

The Romans and Hadrian's Wall

The Roman expansion north reached the Tyne valley around AD80, spreading into lands at that time controlled by the Celtic tribes. Under Agricola, the new governor of Britain, forts were established at Corbridge (Cortopitium) and Chesterholme (Vindolanda) linked by the supply route to Stanegate. Agricola pushed his main military route northwards along the line of what became Dere Street with further forts at High Rochester (Bremenium) and Chew Green. A second route branched off a few miles north of Corbridge to the mouth of the River Tweed, known as the Devil's Causeway.

By AD84 Agricola reached as far north as the Spey valley in Scotland, but withdrew three years later to south of the Forth-Clyde isthmus. Over the next twenty years the Romans gradually abandoned southern Scotland and Stanegate, running between present day Carlisle and Newcastle, became the northernmost frontier of the Roman Empire.

Under Emperor Hadrian in AD122 it was decided to construct a wall to protect this frontier. Hadrian's Wall runs 73 miles (117km) across the narrowest part of England, and was maintained by the Romans for nearly 300 years. The Wall was originally planned to be 15 Roman feet high and 10 Roman feet wide, but it is not known how high the Wall eventually was, or whether there was a parapet or patrol walk along the top. This may not have been necessary

Hadrian's Wall in the snow

because milecastles were built every Roman mile (1480 metres) to house troops, and turrets, which were used as signalling towers, were constructed between each pair of milecastles.

The Wall was constructed using well-shaped facing stones infilled with puddled earth and clay. A ditch was built on the north side, and on the south side another more impressive ditch known as the vallum was constructed. This steep-sided, wide-bottomed boundary ditch owes its name to a mistranslation by the Venerable Bede in his *Ecclesiastical History of the English Nation* (731).

Shortly after work began on the Wall it was decided to move the main fighting force on to the Wall itself, where the troops were housed in sixteen forts. The Wall was also narrowed from 10 to 8 Roman feet (3 to 2.4m), and at many of the surviving sections the narrow wall can be seen to have been built on the original broad foundations. The larger forts would have housed around 1000 infantry or 500 cavalry and would have included barrack blocks, commandant's house, headquarters, granaries, workshops and latrines. Many of the forts within the central section of the Wall are well preserved, including Housesteads, dramatically set on Great Whin Sill overlooking Broomlee Lough. This contains the only visible example of a Roman hospital in Britain and is famous for its wonderfully preserved latrines, featured in nearly every child's textbook on Roman Britain.

During the fifth century, as the collapse of Roman Empire saw the withdrawal of Roman troops under Emperor Honorius, the Wall and its associated forts and civilian settlements become derelict. This was followed by a period of upheaval, with the migration and settlement of new Germanic tribes in Northumberland.

Early Christianity – the Golden Age of Northumbria

These new invading tribes of 'warrior farmers' called themselves Angles or Saxons, and later English. They first occupied the east and south coastal areas and then seem to have penetrated and settled the fertile river valleys. Upland areas were not suited to arable farming and remained heavily defended by native British Celts. In 547AD the Angle chieftain Ida won control of the coastal fortress of Din Guoary, later Bamburgh, and established a new northern kingdom called Bernicia. Anglican control gradually spread over the north and under King Aethelfrith, Bernica and the neighbouring kingdom of Deira were united, creating the kingdom of Northumbria which stretched from the Humber and Forth estuaries.

King Aethelfrith was succeeded by King Edwin, who married a Christian princess from Kent, Ethburge. Edwin was baptised in 627 in York and in doing so brought Christianity to the north. Close to the royal palace at Ad Gefrin, St Paulinus is said to have baptised converts in the River Glen for thirty-six days. After Edwin's death, the kingdom of Northumbria fell apart against the might of the pagan King Cadwallon and the Mercian Prince Penda. Cadwallan was finally defeated and killed at the Battle of Heavensfield, close to Hexham, in 634 by King Oswald. Oswald (the son of Athelfrith) was later canonised. One of Oswald's first acts was to ask the Scottish elders on Iona for a bishop to restore Christianity to the kingdom. St Aidan arrived in 635 and established an Episcopal see on the island of Lindisfarne. It was the beginning of a great flowering of Anglo-Saxon Christianity characterised by scholarship and artistic creativity, perhaps best epitomised by the *Lindisfarne Gospels*.

From the monastery at Lindisfarne missionary monks travelled throughout Northumbria preaching the gospel. Lindisfarne monks were involved in the conversion of Scotland and Mercia and went to the Continent to convert the Germanic tribes. It was to Northumbria that the rulers of mainland Europe sent for books and men to help reform their churches. By the end of the 7th century, stone churches began to be built throughout Northumberland – including one in Hexham by St Wilfrid which was also to become an important centre of learning and Episcopal seat. Elsewhere preaching crosses richly carved with Christian imagery were erected, such as that found in Rothbury.

The most famous of the bishops of Lindisfarne was St Cuthbert (c.630-687), a renowned preacher and ascetic. A few years after his death it was decided to rebury his body in a more prominent position within Lindisfarne Abbey and it was found that his corpse had been miraculously preserved. A shrine was created in honour of St Cuthbert and Lindisfarne became a centre of pilgrimage. In 793 Lindisfarne was brutally attacked and pillaged by the Vikings and in 873, following further coastal raids by the Danes, the monks fled the island carrying the preserved corpse of St Cuthbert. They also took the head of St Oswald, who had been slain at Maserfelth fighting against Penda of Mercia and the Britons of Powys in 642. It was the beginning of an astonishing eleven-year journey around Northumberland in which St Cuthbert's body was carried from place to place, until finally settling in Chester-le-Street and later in Durham. The many crags and hills bearing the diminutive of his name, such as Cuddy's Crag, and the churches dedicated to St Cuthbert are said to be the places where the monks rested whilst carrying his body.

By the end of the 10th century, under constant attack from the Vikings and the Scots in the north, the kingdom of Northumbria had declined to an earldom acknowledging allegiance to the West Saxon kings. Many of its monasteries had been abandoned and its people were impoverished.

The Normans

In 1069 William the Conqueror arrived in York to put down a northern rebellion. Following his victory he laid waste the lands between York and Durham and destroyed every town but Bamburgh, causing a terrible famine and leaving Northumberland a virtual desert for nearly a decade. In the meantime William imposed a strict rule over northern England, introducing new taxes and a feudal system based on service to the king using his own barons and knights. This new warrior aristocracy with families such as the Nevilles, Percys and Mowbrays was to dominate the subsequent history of Northumberland. The imposing of Norman rule was accompanied between 1069 and 1150 by a period of castle building that included the constructions of motte and baileys at Elsdon, Norham and Prudhoe.

William appointed a Norman Earl of Northumberland to look after his interests and within the troubled border hills granted liberties or franchises to barons where the king's writ did not run and no military service was rendered. These included the liberties of Hexham and Redesdale, followed in the 12th century by north and south Tynedale. The family of de Umfravilles held the Liberty of Redesdale and Upper Coquetdale.

Wark on Tyne was the capital of the Liberty of Tynedale, which included the whole of the two Tyne valleys north and west of Hexham. Tynedale was carved out of the old Earldom of Northumberland and came under the lordship of King David of Scotland in the early 12th century. In 1157 King Malcolm of Scotland, whose brother held the Earldom of Northumberland, surrendered the county to Henry II. By way of compensation King Henry then granted Tynedale as a liberty with extensive rights to William, who afterwards became William the Lyon, King of Scotland (1165-1214). Tynedale remained in Scottish hands until 1296 when Edward I deprived John Balliol of it. When Robert the Bruce raided the northern counties in 1314 after Bannockburn, he made the men of Tynedale do homage to him in a bid to reclaim the rights of his predecessors.

The other powerful force which emerged after the Norman Conquest was the growth in political influence of the Church, which remained until the dissolution of the monasteries in 1536 under Henry VIII. Under Norman patronage new monasteries were founded with large areas of land. The most powerful was the bishopric of Durham, which in Northumberland held lands around the River Tweed centred on Norham and Lindisfarne, and around the lower Blyth and Wansbeck valleys where they assumed responsibility for the administration of secular law and order. The Abbey at Hexham controlled much of Hexhamshire whilst Newminster, founded 1157, became one of the largest Cistercian houses in Northern England. It gradually acquired most of Upper Coquetdale, which was granted to them by the de Umfraville lords of Redesdale and Harbottle.

Between 1150 and 1300, peaceful conditions in Northumberland saw an increase in the population that encouraged the colonisation of new land in the upland areas. The characteristic cultivation terraces of this period are known as ridge and furrow or lynchets. These can still be seen on the southern-facing slopes on the sides of the Cheviot Hills around Ingram and Wooler. Many villages with place names containing the suffixes 'hams', 'tons', 'steads' date from this time when new churches were built or existing ones remodelled and expanded. This prosperity was to come to an abrupt end around 1300 with the start of the Border Wars, widespread crop failure and the coming of the Black Death in 1348. The population rapidly declined and many villages and land on the edge of the fells were abandoned. It was to be the middle of the 18th century before Northumberland was recover its economic prosperity.

The Border Troubles

The death of King Alexander III of Scotland in 1286 led to a dispute over the succession to the Scottish throne, enabling Edward I of England to engineer the ascension of the puppet king, John Balliol. Balliol's subsequent attempt to negotiate an alliance with the French spurred King Edward to march north. He crushed Balliol and left Scotland under a governing English army. It was a short-lived victory. Under William Wallace the Scots retaliated, sending raiding parties into Northumberland and laying large areas of the county to waste. The victory of Robert the Bruce over Edward II at Bannockburn ensured the independence of Scotland in 1314, but for the next three hundred years there was continuous strife between the two countries. Battles such as those at Otterburn, Flodden Field and Haildon Hill led by the earls and lords of Scotland and England saw the death of hundreds of brave men. These were celebrated in the border ballads such as the *Ballad of Chevy Chase* and *The Battle of Otterburn*. These were later popularised by Sir Walter Scott in the *Child Ballads*.

Throughout this period, raiding and hostage-taking either side of the Border intensified animosity between the two nations, which was mirrored by local blood feuds between families and clans or 'surnames' such as the Charltons, Dodds, Potts and Fletchers. Edward I had instituted a new form of government for the English side of the border following his invasion of Scotland in which the Wardens of the Marches were made responsible for defence and the enforcement of Marcher Law. This was to remain in force throughout the Border troubles. In effect this meant that the northern parts of Northumberland and Cumberland became military zones with Cumberland forming the West March, Northumberland the East March. By the end of the 14th century, the East March was subdivided. The new East March was based at Berwick and included the coastal plain north of the River Aln, while the Middle March included the whole of the English Cheviots, Coquetdale, Redesdale and North Tyne valley and was centred in Hexham. A similar system was established on the Scottish side of the border. The lords of the Wardens were responsible for justice and retribution and would set a day of truce to hold a joint court to settle disputes. Often these meetings would be held in remote passes or gates such as Carter Bar to prevent treachery, though many such meetings still ended in bloody confrontation.

Despite the Union of Crowns in 1603, throughout the 16th and 17th centuries Northumberland remained a violent society. Constant warfare and raiding had devastated large parts of it, and the ancient custom of Gravelkind, where upon a man's death his land was divided between his sons, created plots of land too small to be viable. Faced with too many mouths to feed and too little food or employment, bands of men took what they wanted by reiving or cattle stealing, preying both on their neighbours and on rival kinship groups across the border. The reputation of the Middle March, and in particular Tynedale and Redesdale was notorious, inhabited by "wild misdemeaned people". The Wardens of the Marches only had limited success in dealing with the endemic thieving, and some simply turned a blind eye. Those involved in reiving were well aware of the death penalty if caught and so every raid was carefully planned. Most attacks were carried out at night when there was no moon. Typically a raiding party would consist of between 50 and 200 men on horseback, each man equipped with a steel cap or bonnet and a leather coat sewn with plates of metal or horn.

The legacy of fortified buildings found in Northumberland starkly illustrates the history of continual strife against the Scots and the lawless and violent society that emerged in its wake. One of the most distinctive features found either side of the border are the pele towers built by the lesser gentry to protect their stock and dependants. These tower houses were originally built of timber within a barmkin or timber-fenced enclosure, but by the 14th century the towers were built of stone, often with walls 3-4ft thick. These pele towers were usually three storeys high with a stone-vaulted ground floor which served as a storeroom or even as a refuge for livestock. The normal access to the first floor was by an external ladder or a stone staircase that led to the main living quarters and chamber above. Henry V made a list of such towers in 1415, which included over eighty pele towers, including vicars' peles. Many pele towers are still standing, often in ruins. Others have been altered and incorporated into later buildings.

Bastle houses were built by farmers in the remote uplands from around 1540. The majority were within twenty miles of the border. They tend to be sited in clusters or within easy reach of their neighbours. These defensive farmhouses consist of two storeys with pitched gables. The walls on the ground floor are generally about 4ft thick and have an entrance door for cattle and other stock and ventilation slits. The entrance to the upper floor and the family's living quarters was by a retrievable wooden ladder which only later would have been replaced by an outside stone stair. Most bastles were originally roofed with heather thatch, which was later replaced by slate. The remains of bastles can be found mostly in Redesdale, North Tynedale and Coquetdale. Some are roofless and in ruins while others have been adapted to be used as farmhouses or cottages. Two of the most impressive surviving bastles are Black Middens near Greenhaugh and Woodhouse Bastle near Holystone.

A Civilised Landscape

Throughout the late 17th and 18th centuries, security increased and

Northumberland began to be slowly transformed. New wealth was created by the agrarian reform that began to revolutionise the farmsteads of rural Northumberland. Fields were enclosed with hedges or drystone walls, new breeds of sheep and cattle were introduced and new crops developed. Landowners and the lesser gentry began to build more comfortable houses. This trend culminated in the elegant country houses designed by architects such as Paine, Vanbrugh and Robert Adam, and in the 19th century by the energetic John Dobson of Newcastle. By the mid-18th century, inspired by Northumberland-born landscape gardener Lancelot 'Capability' Brown, many of the large estates were transformed into elegant parkland with lakes and planted woodland. New estate villages like Cambo or Capheaton were built or, in some cases, relocated, to house the estate workers and labourers.

Although some of Northumberland's roads have ancient origins it was only in the 18th and 19th centuries that a coherent road pattern emerged through the agency of turnpike trusts. Between 1747 and 1826, nineteen trusts oversaw the building of various trunk roads including the Great North Road and the Hexham to Alnmouth Corn Road. Many of Northumberland's towns and villages owe their growth to their position on a major thoroughfare, with towns like Morpeth and Belford developing as major staging posts on the Great North Road between Scotland and England.

Lead Mining

For centuries the hills of Northumberland have been quarried for building stone and lime, and mined for lead. The lead mining industry in particular was to have a major impact on the North Pennines landscape. In Northumberland the North Pennine orefield included the East Allen valley based around the village of Allenheads; West Allendale centred on Coalcleugh and the Derwent Valley around Blanchland. Between 1729 and 1896, the upper valleys of the East and West Allen valleys yielded over a quarter of a million tons of lead-bearing ore, known as galena, that had been found in the various Pennine limestones.

Lead was primarily worked in levels running into the hillside rather than in shafts, and the entrance to these litter the hillsides. Hushes or scars can also still be seen on the moors where an area was temporarily dammed with water which was then released to scour the hillside and expose the lead veins in the underlying rocks. Water-power played an important part in the process of washing and crushing the lead ore, and throughout the North Pennine valleys reservoirs and the remains of river weirs can be found. Once crushed the lead ore was roasted in smelt mills to produce pigs of lead, each weighing around 63kgs, to be carried by packhorse and later by road for sale in Newcastle. During the early 19th century long, horizontal flues were constructed to take the noxious fumes from the smelt mill to the moors above. They also allowed any vaporised lead to be recovered, by sending men to scrape the walls. Often these flues, built of stone forming an arched tunnel on the hillside, were more than half a mile long. From Allen Mill at Catton the flue system extends nearly five miles. Lead mining was exceedingly labour intensive and at its height most of the population of the Allendales and upper Derwent valleys were dependent directly or indirectly on lead mining.

Coal Mining and the Railways

It was coal that was to lie at the heart of the North East's industrial development and this was based around the South Northumberland and Durham coalfields. Changes in the coal industry such as the gradual introduction of more effective pumping and winding machinery saw the development in the 18th and early 19th centuries of much larger and deeper pits. The Newcomen engine, which enabled water to be pumped from mines quickly, was widely adopted by the mine owners of Northumberland. The other important innovations pioneered in Northumberland were the use of horse-drawn waggonways and, later, steam-powered engines to carry coal from the pits to navigable water. The coming of the age of steam was to have a major impact on social and industrial development, particularly of south-east Northumberland. In a triangle stretching from the River Tyne to the mouth of the Coquet at Amble, thriving coal and shipbuilding industries dominated the lives of the new communities like Ashington Newbiggin and Blyth that had been built around the new mines, ports and harbours. Whilst coal mining, shipbuilding and many of their support industries are no more in Northumberland, the majority of its population still continues to live in the south-east of the county.

Northumberland Today

The beauty and unspoilt nature of Northumberland's landscape is recognised through the designation of a National Park, an Area of Outstanding Natural Beauty (AONB) and a Heritage Coastline within its boundaries. Beyond the once industrial south-east triangle, Northumberland remains predominantly rural, farming country, despite the challenges facing both the upland and arable farmer. Unlike so many other scenic landscapes, its very remoteness has protected Northumberland from the excesses of tourism. This is not a county of tea shops, gift and craft shops, which so often seem to dominate rural communities. In Northumberland the character of the villages and towns remains surprisingly unchanged. Here the churches, ancient tracks and simple stone cottages set in an often remote and lonely countryside still provide a glimpse of the lives and experience of the generations of ordinary people who shaped the landscape of modern day Northumberland.

The Towns and Villages

ACOMB [Tynedale]

NY9366: 1½ miles (2.5km) NNE of Hexham

Acomb is built along a side road to the east of the A6079, above the confluence of the North and South Tyne rivers. Now a popular commuter village, Acomb was once a lead-mining centre. The old village is no more than a single street of 18th-century houses standing around a pleasant square marked by a Victorian drinking fountain.

St John of Beverley stands just south of the village amongst trees and close to the site of the former 7th-century hermitage of the same name. Built by the Newcastle architect John Dobson in 1818 and enlarged in the 1880s, the church has a spectacular panelled ceiling and carved screen. On the outside walls of the church stand an uninscribed Roman altar which has been converted into a sundial, a boulder decorated with ancient cup and ring markings and a fine 14th-century marble slab inscribed with Lombardic script.

ALLENDALE TOWN [Tynedale]

NY8355: 5½ miles (9km) S of Haydon Bridge

This once prosperous 19th-century lead-mining town stands high above the wooded gorge of the East Allen river. Solid grey houses line Allendale's broad, tree-lined main street, and grouped around the square is a fine collection of coaching inns and former Temperance Hotels. The Temperance Hotels are testament to the strong Nonconformist tradition in the North Pennines and the belief that milk was an effective antidote to lead poisoning. The lead-mining industry reached its zenith in the area in the 18th and 19th centuries but cheaper imports killed it off in the 1920s. The surrounding moors still contain the redundant lead workings and associated buildings, now in ruins. The clean moorland air and natural beauty of the area also made Allendale Town a popular health resort with Edwardian day-trippers, who arrived by train. The town is still popular with walkers and cyclists who come to enjoy the surrounding countryside.

St Cuthbert's Church is rather austere. It overlooks the river and dates from 1807. Alterations were made in 1874. It has an attractive carved lych-gate and an interesting sundial of 1842 on its south wall. The sundial celebrates Allendale's claim to be the geographical centre of Britain at a latitude of 54 degrees 50 minutes, midway between Cape Wrath and Beachy Head.

Below the church is the portal of **Blackett's Level,** which was started in 1854. This was an ambitious attempt to drain the mines of the whole valley and was intended to be 7 miles (11km) long. It eventually reached 4½ miles (7km), but was never completed. It was used until 1903 when the Allenheads mine closed.

The annual Allendale Show is held on a pretty riverside site on the outskirts of the town in late summer, but it is for the '**Tar Barling**' or Allendale Fire Festival that the town is best known. This festival is held on New Year's Eve and a group of men with blackened faces and dressed in strange costumes, the 'festival guisers', carry blazing barrels of tar on their heads through the town. This parade of fire culminates in a massive bonfire in the market place.

ALLENHEADS [Tynedale]

NY8645: 7 miles (11km) S of Allendale Town

A sleepy estate village at the head of the East Allen valley, Allenheads was once the centre of the North Pennines' lead-mining industry. The local mines produced a sixth of Britain's lead. The largest silver mine in the world was also here until its closure in 1896. With the village in serious decline in the mid-1980s, a Village Trust was formed to spearhead efforts to regenerate the village based on the area's rich industrial heritage. A former coaching inn is now the **Allenheads Heritage Centre** and is managed by the local community. It houses an exhibition describing the history of this former lead-mining village.

In the centre of the village is a restored Armstrong hydraulic engine. Powered by water, it was used down one of the mine shafts to pump water until the 1940s. Other reminders of the village's industrial past include the remains of the bouse team, or series of stone ore bunkers, the 19th-century estate offices and miners' terraces and the entrance to the horse track, a spiral incline descending into the deep mines below the village. Various trails have been developed which explore the industrial archaeology of the village and the surrounding hillsides, including the various reservoirs used to store the water used for washing and preparing the ore and the site of the smelting mill at Dirt Pot. In addition there is also a short but excellent 700-metre nature trail marked with attractive information boards which follows the wooded valley of the River Allen.

The Beaumont family who owned the mineral rights to the area built Allenheads Hall in 1847. The hall was used by Thomas Sopwith, mine agent and engineer for the Beamount-Blackett family between 1845 and 1871 and architect of many of the more ambitious engineering schemes within the valley to improve the efficiency of the mines. Instead of rose beds, the hall's garden had little mounds of purple fluorspar and white quartz crystals from the mines beneath.

ALNHAM [Alnwick]

NT9911: 7 miles (11km) NW of Rothbury

Alnham is set in the remote Upper Aln valley and the surrounding hills contain the remains of prehistoric hill forts, old field systems, cairns and hut sites and ancient packhorse and drovers' tracks. Alnham is a typical Northumberland hamlet based on a 15th-century vicar's pele tower and Norman church. The pele tower, with its walls 6ft thick, has been beautifully restored and is now a private house. During the Border Raids the ground floor would have been used for storage while the occupants lived upstairs for safety in the event of an attack. On the hillside facing the pele tower is a mound that was once the site of ancient castle. The Scotts of Teviotdale probably burned it in 1532. The castle would have guarded the gateway to the fertile Vale of Whittingham at the southern end of the ancient Salters' Road.

St Michael and All Angels predominantly dates from the 13th century, though Saxon quoins are to be seen in the eastern corners of the nave. By the mid-19th century the church was in ruins. It was rebuilt in 1870 after the ravages of time and a declining population had led to its neglect. Little now remains from medieval times apart from some 13th-century gravestones on the floor with carved swords and floral crosses. One also bears a pair of sheaves, a traditional symbol for a woman.

Castle Hill stands three-quarters of a mile (1km) west. It was a well defended hill fort when built around 2500 years ago, with deep defences and ramparts. A Romano-British settlement was later built over it. It provides wonderful views of the Cheviot and Simonside Hills.

At **High Knowles,** on the summit of the hill just off the road, there are traces of a more ancient palisaded circular settlement dating from the middle of the first millennium BC. On a lower knoll is a smaller settlement consisting of around sixteen buildings.

ALNMOUTH [Alnwick]

NU2410: 4 miles (6km) SE of Alnwick

Set on a south-facing peninsula, a row of pretty, colour-washed houses follows the curve of the estuary of the River Aln beside one of the most beautiful beaches in England. Alnmouth was described by John Wesley in 1748 as 'a small sea-port famous for all kinds of wickedness'. Today it is a quiet seaside resort with an attractive jumble of red-roofed, grey stone-built houses, inns and shops.

The village was founded as a port between 1207 and 1208 and became a prosperous shipbuilding centre and grain port. Several houses in the village are converted granaries and the road leading to the village was a turnpike road once known as Corn Road Harbour. During the American War of Independence, the notorious pirate Paul Jones tried to bombard the harbour, but the great storm on Christmas Day 1806 had a much greater impact. It changed the course of the river, cutting the medieval church from the village, and caused the harbour to silt up, bringing the rapid decline of the port.

Just south, facing the village, is a grassy hill which was the site of the Norman church of **St Waleric,** the remains of which were washed away by the storm of 1806. Its roots go back to the earliest days of Christianity's arrival in Northumbria. Two pieces of a sculpted shaft of an 8th-century cross were dug up nearby and are now in Alnwick Castle Museum. Alnmouth claims with other places in Northumberland to have been the site of a synod described by Bede as 'Twyford' where Cuthbert was elected Bishop of Hexham in 684. There are also a number of ancient gravestones at the foot of the hill beside a tiny, derelict, 19th-century mortuary chapel in which services were held for seamen.

ALNWICK [Alnwick]

NU1813: 17 miles (27km) N of Morpeth

Alnwick is the ducal town of Northumberland. Strategically placed at a crossing of the River Aln, the name Alnwick means 'town on the clear water'. Within easy distance of the disputed Scottish border, this handsome town grew up beneath the guardian walls of its castle. In the fourteenth century this became the headquarters of the Percy dynasty, first earls then dukes of Northumberland.

Alnwick was a Saxon and then a Norman settlement. Its present street plan still conforms to that of a medieval village of cottages grouped around a green. It stood at a junction of routes and Bondgate Without, Bondgate Within, Pottergate and Bailiffgate (Baileygate) are all located on very ancient tracks. The intimate, cobbled market place is flanked by Northumberland Hall (1826) and still retains its medieval character, with narrow streets radiating from it and a market cross and stone *pant* (a stone structure covering a well) in one corner. The town has long been an important commercial centre; its market charter was granted in 1291. A market is still held here and the annual week-long Alnwick Fair is a costumed re-enactment of a medieval fair.

Between Bondgate Within and Bondgate Without is the imposing Hotspur Gate, the only surviving gateway of the original four that were part of the town's defensive walls. These were built following the plunder of the town by the Scots in 1428. For a long time Hotspur Gate was used as the county gaol. The tower at Pottergate is a replica built in 1768 as part of the improvements made by the first duke.

The first Duke of Northumberland was a notable improver. He led the way by rebuilding much of the castle, the estate farms and parts of the town, including the town hall (1731) in Fenkle Street. In 1773 he replaced the medieval bridge over the River Aln with the elegant Lion Bridge, designed by John Adam and adorned with a cast-lead Percy Lion. During this period many of the town's houses were replaced with the fine classical residences which now line Market Street, Narrow Gate and Bondgate.

Alnwick has always been an important staging post for travellers between Scotland and England, and at one time contained over fifty inns. The Nag's Head in Fenkle Street has been catering for travellers since the 16th century. The 17th-century Old Cross Inn in Narrowgate is better known as 'Dirty Bottles' after the row of bottles lying in the window which have remained untouched for almost 200 years, after allegedly being cursed. The inn got its name from an old stone cross that was once over its entrance. The cross is said to have been stolen from Alnwick Abbey and erected at night – upside down!

From the centre of Alnwick, the castle is barely visible. Only from the Lion Bridge can you get a real sense of its size, strength and superb defensive position. **Alnwick Castle** is of Saxon origin, although the current building dates from the 11th century. The Percys acquired it in 1309 and were responsible for much of its development. The castle was carefully restored in the 18th century, when the surrounding parkland was landscaped by Capability Brown for the first Duke. The fourth Duke employed Anthony Salvin to undertake further restoration work in the mid-1800s and created a sumptuous Italian Renaissance-style interior. In essence the castle now consists of a central keep on a mound surrounded by beautifully kept lawns within a curtain wall strengthened by a series of towers and turrets. An unusual feature is the 14th-century barbican whose battlements are lined with stone figures representing armed warriors repelling an attack. James Johnson of Stamfordham carved the statues in the mid-1800s, but they are thought to be based on original stone figures. The keep is entered over a wooden bridge, which would once have been a drawbridge over a moat. This now rugged medieval exterior is in sharp contrast to its lavish Victorian interior complete with fine 18th-century furniture, a renowned collection of Meissen porcelain and a wealth of paintings by Canalletto, Van Dyck and Titian.

The fourth Duke was interested in early history and the **Antiquities Museum** in the Postern Tower contains many local artefacts dating from pre-Roman times. The Abbots Tower (1309) now houses the **Royal Northumberland Fusiliers Regimental Museum.** Raised as an Irish regiment in 1674, the Regiment's history includes the American War of Independence, the 1991 Gulf conflict and Bosnia. Alnwick Castle, its grounds and museums are open to the public throughout the summer months.

At the eastern entrance of the town is a 25.3-metre (83ft) tower surmounted by the lion symbol of the Percys with four recumbent lions at its base. An internal staircase leads to a balcony at the top of the tower. It was built in 1816 as a gift from the ducal estate tenants after the Duke of Northumberland reduced their rents during the Napoleonic Wars. It is known as the **Percy Tenantry Column** or Farmers' Folly, perhaps because the Duke was so surprised at the obvious wealth of his tenants that he increased the rents again!

The **parish church of St Michael** is Norman in origin but was rebuilt in Perpendicular style in the 14th century. It is one of the finest Gothic churches in the north, despite being restored in 1781 and again in 1831 by Salvin. The chancel pillars are particularly fine, topped with richly carved foliage and fruit. One is known as the Hotspur and is carved with the crescents and fetterlocks that became the symbol of the Percys. In the west wall of north aisle, one window contains 15th-century glass roundels depicting a pelican and a girl's head. One unusual feature is a polygonal turret in the south-east corner of the church. This was used as the vicar's lodgings, and later as an observation post as late as the Napoleonic Wars. The church contains one of the finest early 14th-century Flemish chests in the country. It is made of oak and carved with hunting scenes and dragons. In the tower and by the porch there are a number of interesting 13th-century gravestones carved with various symbols including a hunting horn, shears and a key. Among the various monuments and effigies there is one small statue thought to be King Henry VI and another of a near-naked saint bound with ropes and shot with arrows, which is either St Sebastian or the Northumbrian St Maurice who was martyred by the Danes.

In the parkland north of the town is Abbeylands, part of the castle park. Just below Canongate Bridge are the scant riverside remains of **Alnwick Abbey**. It was founded in 1147 by Eustace Fitz-John for twenty-one Premonstratensian canons. The only remaining building is the 15th-century gatehouse. The abbey once owned two important relics: the chalice of Thomas of Canterbury and the toe of Simon de Montfort, whose body was hacked to pieces at the Battle of Evesham in 1265. This toe was reputed to have great curative powers.

To the north of Abbeylands is **Malcolm's Cross,** marking the spot where Malcolm Cranmore, King of Scotland, was murdered in 1093 by Arkle Moreal. Moreal was the steward of Robert Mowbray, the last in his line to bear the title Earl of Northumberland. Elizabeth, Duchess of Northumberland, erected the present cross in 1774. It is not known whether Malcolm was besieging Alnwick or returning from a visit to William Rufus at Gloucester. Close by are the ruins of St Leonard's Hospital, which was founded between 1193 and 1216 by Eustace de Vescy for the benefit of the souls of murdered Malcolm and St Margaret, his wife.

Stretching north-west of the town on both sides of the River Aln is **Hulne Park**. It is part of the Alnwick Castle estate and in the 18th century it became something of a pleasure garden for the Percys and was landscaped by Lancelot 'Capability' Brown and Robert Adam. On the northern side of the river are the remains of a monastic house, Hulne Priory, a fortified abbey established by the Carmelite order of White Friars in 1242. It was founded by William de Vesci and is among the best preserved friaries in England. The friary is surrounded by a massive 15th-century curtain wall that is still standing almost intact to a height of 3.6 metres (12ft). The fourth Earl of Northumberland also built a defensive tower in 1488 as a place of refuge from raiding Scots. It has an oriel window looking towards Scotland. Linked to the tower by a bridge is a beautiful Gothic summer house which was built in 1778-9 as part of the landscaping of the park. Parts of the 13th-century friary building still remain, including the narrow priory church which contains an unusual triple sedilia (priests' seats) and sacristy where it is thought the bread for Holy Communion was prepared in a large recess.

From the priory there is an attractive a 1¾-mile (3km) riverside and forest walk to **Brizlee Tower,** which crowns the wooded hilltop. This ornate tower was built by the first Duke of Northumberland, Hugh, possibly to his own design but more likely that of Robert Adam in 1781. Below the lower balcony is a relief portrait of the duke with a Latin inscription. This translates as, 'Look around! I myself have measured out all these things; they are of my ordering, my design; many of these trees have been planted by my own hand.' The tower is 24 metres (78ft) tall, and it is said that from the upper balcony on a clear day seven castles can be seen – Warkworth, Alnwick, Bamburgh, Holy Island, Chillingham and the ruins of Dunstanburgh and Ros Castle, the Iron Age hill fort.

ALWINTON [Alnwick]

NT9206: 9 miles (15km) NW of Rothbury

Alwinton is a small village in Coquetdale and beautifully situated beneath the Cheviot foothills, facing south to the Harbottle hills. It lies on the crossroads of a number of ancient routes. Its few pretty stone cottages and pub, the Rose and Crown, stand on one side of the village green, overlooking Hosedon Burn. Sir Walter Scott stayed at the pub whilst researching *Rob Roy*.

Clennel Street, an ancient moorland track, climbs steeply above the hills above Alwinton to Cocklawfoot at the head of Bowmount Water in Scotland, a distance of 12½ miles. Cairns and earthworks mark its route and its name evokes the landscape it crosses: clean hills without natural woodland. The track pre-dates the Romans and was used by generations of cattle drovers, shepherds and pedlars.

St Michael's Church is situated below the village on the south side of the River Coquet. It is an interesting and unusual building, primarily because its hillside position necessitates a ten-step rise from the nave to the chancel. Founded in the 12th century, St Michael's was substantially altered in 1851.

An annual **Shepherd's Show** is held on the second Saturday in October. It is the last agricultural show of the Border

Alwinton

Valleys and one of the most colourful. Begun in 1874 to encourage good stock husbandry, horticulture and dog training, the Alwinton Show has remained a popular local event and includes fell racers, stick carvers, crafts, wrestlers and Northumbrian pipes.

At **Camp Knowe** on the hillside opposite Alwinton village are the ramparts and ditches of a prehistoric hill fort. **Chew Green** stands at the top of the Coquet valley, amidst the desolate moorland of the Cheviot Hills and 8 miles (13km) west of Alwinton. Here are the remains of a Roman military camp which the Romans called Ad Fines ('the end of the world'). Chew Green was a staging post on the Roman road Dere Street and was strategically sited to enable any attacking forces from the north to be seen from afar. It consists of a remarkable series of earthworks that include early marching camps, ramparts and a smaller second fort. The best place to see these earthworks is from the road on the Saddle between Harden Edge and Thirlmoor, which provides a bird's-eye view of the site (access is dependent on the Army Training Area being open).

ANCROFT [Berwick upon Tweed]

NU0045: 5 miles (8km) S of Berwick upon Tweed

A row of long, low cottages with red-tiled roofs lines the road which curves through the tiny hamlet of Ancroft. The Norman church of St Anne, which has one of the finest pele towers in Northumberland, dominates over the scene. The tower was added around 1300 to shelter the villagers from attack by Border raiders. Close to the church are the remains of a much larger village that was destroyed after the plague in 1667. A green field sloping down to Dean Burn is known as Broomie Huts. This derives from the time when those suffering from the plague were carried here from the village and a bower of broom placed over each. After death the body and the broom were burnt together.

AKELD [Berwick upon Tweed]

NT9529: 3 miles (5km) NW of Wooler

Set within this tiny hamlet below Humbleton Hill is a good example of a 16th-century bastle house. These were built for protection against the Border raiders so accommodation for the family was provided above, accessed by a ladder, and the stock were kept below. Akeld was once a fair-sized village, but after land changes in the 19th century it became a large farm with labourers' cottages. All the farm buildings have now been converted into luxury holiday accommodation.

Close by on the main road and opposite Humbleton Hill is a monument and plaque on the site of the Saxon town **Ad Gefrin.** In the 7th century the kings of Northumbria lived in this royal township. The missionary Paulinus is said to have baptised converts in the nearby River Glen in AD627.

AMBLE [Alnwick]

NU2604: 7½ miles (12km) SE of Alnwick

Picturesquely sited at the mouth of the Coquet, Amble was little more than a hamlet before the construction of its harbour (originally known as Warksworth Harbour) between 1838 and 39. The town owes its growth and prosperity to the 19th-century coalfields from which it used to export coal, but as this trade declined so did the fortunes of the town. The development of an award-winning marina on the site of the former staithes has brought new life to the town and it is once again a busy harbour town.

Coquet Island and its lighthouse lies a mile offshore. It is now a Royal Society for the Protection of Birds (RSPB) reserve for thousands of puffins, terns, eider ducks and for the roseate tern, one of Britain's rarest seabirds. Boat trips around the island are organised by the RSPB from the harbour at Amble. The unusual square-towered lighthouse is owned by Duke of Northumberland and was built in 1841 on the site of a Benedictine monastery. One of the first keepers was William Darling, brother of the heroine Grace Darling. The lighthouse used to be staffed by three keepers but is now automatic. Its fog warning is still known as the Coquet gun. St Cuthbert is said to have visited Coquet Island in 684 to grant an interview with Elfleda, Abbess of Whitby, at which St Cuthbert accepted the position of Bishop of Lindisfarne.

Amble Dunes is a local nature reserve south of the town. Its tall, narrow sand dunes are typical of those along the Northumberland coast. The best time to explore the reserve is in summer, when the bloody cranesbill, bird's-foot trefoil and burnet rose play host to a range of moths and butterflies, including the common blue and meadow brown. Close by is Low Hauxley Nature Reserve, a former open-cast site which is now a bird sanctuary containing a number of hides.

ASHINGTON [Wansbeck]

NZ2787: 5 miles (8km) E of Morpeth

This major town was built on the Northumbrian coalfield in the mid-19th century. At that time a series of pits were sunk, including 'Fell-em-Doon' shaft, Bothal Pit, Linton Colliery and Woodhorn colliery, and new housing erected in a strict grid-iron pattern. Ashington has become synonymous with leeks and footballers. The rows of turn-of-the-century terraced housing were home to the famous footballing brothers Jack and Bobby Charlton and their uncle, 'Wor Jackie' Milburn of Newcastle United. Wansbeck Riverside Park provides attractive walks along the river and a range of recreational facilities including canoeing and fishing.

AYDON [Tynedale]

NZ0066: 1½ miles (2.5km) NE of Corbridge

On the edge of the tiny village of Aydon, set above the secluded wooded slopes of Cor Burn is a superb example of a medieval fortified manor house. Originally an undefended house, **Aydon Castle** was built by Robert De Reymes, a rich Suffolk merchant who settled here at the end of 13th century, during a period of unusual peace in the Borders. Soon after the troubles resumed, the house was fortified, though it did not prevent it being burnt and pillaged by the Scots in 1315, and then recaptured by the English two years later. Over subsequent years the house had to be continually repaired, leaving the de Reymes family impoverished. Aydon Castle was converted into a farmhouse in the 17th century and lived in until 1960. Throughout this time the building was little altered. It is now in the care of English Heritage and provides an evocative insight into the life of 14th-century lesser nobility. The magnificent Great Hall and Solar (chamber) are particularly fine, with one window decorated with an unusual bearded head.

BAMBURGH [Alnwick]

NU1834: 17 miles (27km) SE of Berwick upon Tweed

Bamburgh's pleasant grey-stone cottages, tearooms, craft shops and fine inns surround a wide, wooded triangular green called The Grove. The whole scene is dominated by the massive walls, keep and towers of Bamburgh Castle, standing on the great dolerite outcrop of Great Whin Sill.

Bamburgh Castle stands 150ft above sea level and extends for a quarter of a mile along the cliff top. The first fortifications date back to Anglo-Saxon times, when the Chieftain Ida built a wooden fort on the rock in AD547. At this time it was the capital of the kingdom of Bernicia. The wife of Ida's grandson, King Ethelfrith, is said to have given the town its name Bebba-burgh, 'Bebba's town'. In AD993 the Vikings destroyed the castle. It was rebuilt by the Normans under Henry II and became a fort of immense strategic importance. For 400 years it was a stronghold of the crown against invading Scots and rebellious barons. Many kings stayed at the castle, including Edward I, Edward II and Edward III, and it was the scene of John Balliol's surrender. During the Wars of the Roses, when under the command of Henry IV, the castle fell to Edward's IV canons, the first English castle to succumb to gunfire. Queen Elizabeth later granted it to the Foster family. In 1893 the castle was bought by the first Lord Armstrong and was converted into a private residence. Still in the ownership of the Armstrong family, the castle is now open to the public.

Bamburgh Castle retains its massive Norman keep with 9-10ft (2.9m) thick walls, but the interior is mainly 19th century. The Kings' Hall is particularly impressive, with a carved teak ceiling and panelled walls. The castle contains an interesting collection of paintings, china and porcelain as well as suits of armour, and various artefacts of local historical interest.

The **parish church of St Aidan** is named after the saint who was called to Northumbria by King Oswald after the Christian victory at Heavensfield near Hexham. Aidan was given the task of resuming the conversion of the country, which had been interrupted by the defeat of the previous monarch by pagans and the flight of the earlier missionaries and St Paulinus. The present church stands on the site of the rudimentary Saxon church of St Aidan's time. According to Bede, it was outside the west wall of that building, under an awning or tent, that St Aidan died on 31st August 651, worn out by his self-imposed austerities and his untiring missionary work. In the present tower is a wooden beam that is said to have supported these awnings. It is supposed to possess miraculous fire-resistant qualities.

The present church has a fine square tower. The 13th-century nave has arcades divided by pointed arches on round columns. Above the south arcade are six unusual openings that were once clerestory windows. The church has an extremely long chancel and alongside the chancel arch is an unusual feature – a squint or hagioscope decorated with 14th-century tracery. This was designed to allow worshippers in the south part of the nave to see the altar. Underneath the chancel floor and discovered quite by accident is a crypt which contained five coffins of the Foster family. It may have been used to exhibit relics associated with St Aidan and St Oswald.

The **Grace Darling Museum** commemorates Grace's heroism in rowing out in a dreadful storm on the night of September 7th 1838 to rescue nine crew members of the steamship *Forfarshire*, which was wrecked on a rock. The museum contains the small fishing coble used in the rescue and various other mementos. A plaque on a cottage beside the castle end of The Grove marks Grace Darling's birthplace and a memorial to her life can be seen in the church and in the churchyard. She died aged twenty-six, of tuberculosis.

Below the castle lies an impressive sandy beach and dune system, part of which is the **Bamburgh Dunes SSSI.** It contains a full range of dune habitats, including wet hollows allowing plants such as the burnet rose and bloody cranesbill to flourish. There are excellent walks from here along the coast to Budle Point and Warren Mill.

BARDON MILL [Tynedale]

NY7864: 4½ miles (7km) E of Haltwhistle

An attractive group of cottages standing on the north bank of the South Tyne form the village, dominated by the Errington Reay and Co. Pottery established in 1878. The pottery is housed in a converted water-powered woollen mill, whose equipment was destroyed by fire in 1876. The pottery used to specialise in salt-glazed sanitary ware and bricks, but today produces a range of ornamental pots. **Crindledikes**, 1½ miles (2.5km) north, is an excellent example of a beautifully preserved limestone kiln. It stands dramatically against the skyline on the edge of a former quarry.

Vindolanda, a mile north of the village and just south of Hadrian's Wall, was the main garrison fort for the Roman Army and the frontier home for 500 Roman soldiers. It is now a museum based in the former 19th-century house of Chesterholm. Excavations have revealed an extensive civilian settlement which include houses, shops, two burial tombs, the regimental bathhouse and a building thought to be the official rest home or inn of the Imperial Post. Most of the buildings date from the last phase of Roman occupation, towards the end of the 4th century.

Some of the most remarkable finds

have been a large number of Roman writing tablets. When translated they have provided a fascinating insight into life in the fort and town, including comments on the condition of the roads, correspondence to centurions and slaves and plans for a birthday party. Over 2000 Roman shoes have been found, alongside textiles, cooking utensils and weapons. These are now displayed in the visitor centre. Alongside the excavated buildings are various reconstructions of sections of Hadrian's Wall, including the turf wall and a turret. There is also a temple set within the attractive grounds around the wooded gorge of Chainley Burn.

BEADNELL [Berwick upon Tweed]

NU2329: 5 miles (8km) SE of Bamburgh

Set against splendid sand dunes and fringed by a belt of trees, the village of Beadnell is best known for its fine 18th-century limekilns preserved by the National Trust. They stand close to the village's tiny fishing harbour, gaunt against the sea and looking like the ruins of a castle. Their archways are now packed with lobster pots.

Just north of the harbour are the remains of the medieval chapel of St Ebba. Its 18th-century successor, with a curious spire rather like a lighthouse, stands in the village. Inside the nave is an attractive and unusual Second World War memorial window depicting the bearded figure of Oswald, King of Northumbria holding a chalice on which a raven is perched. Behind him is his sister, St Ebba, holding a crook.

BEDLINGTON [Wansbeck]

NZ2581: 4 miles (6.5km) W of Blyth

Bedlington retains its mining-village character, though prior to the sinking of the first mine in 1840 it had a history going back to medieval times. It was once the capital of the area known as Bedlingtonshire, which formed part of the County Palatine of Durham. At its centre is a long, wide main street called Front Street. This is lined with square, brownish-stone houses and shops and much of it is designated a conservation area. It was here that the rails for the Stockton and Darlington railway were first cast. The town is also the birthplace of Daniel Gooch (1816-89), the famous Great Western Railway engineer. Bedlington is also home of the famous terriers, originally bred for badger baiting.

St Cuthbert's is basically a late Norman church with a fine carved chancel arch with zigzag moulding. Inside is a stone inscribed Watson's Wake. It is in memory of somnambulist Cuthbert Watson, who fell to his death in 1669 after someone woke him with a shout while he was climbing the building.

Bedlington Country Park is just outside the town and provides five miles of woodland walks and nature trails on the banks of the River Blyth. **Plessey Woods Country Park** is known locally as Bluebell Woods. People have come to enjoy the woods around the banks of the River Blyth for generations. There are more than 40 hectares (100 acres) of woodland, meadow and riverside and they are home to a range of wildlife including woodpeckers, nuthatches, dippers and kingfishers as well as red squirrel, roe deer and otters. During the 18th century the woods were managed as coppice and used to produce corf (or wicker) to make baskets for hauling coal out of the local mines.

Earth Balance, at nearby Bomarsund, is a brand new attraction devoted to sustainable development. Powered by a fully integrated, renewable energy system including wind, water and short rotation coppice, the site includes an organic bakery, nature reserve, aviary, reed-bed system and exhibitions.

BELLINGHAM [Tynedale]

NY8383: 14 miles (22km) NW of Hexham

Bellingham is the ancient capital of the North Tyne valley. This peaceful little market town is an important centre for the smaller communities and isolated farms throughout the North Tyne and Upper Rede valleys. Each autumn Bellingham hosts the annual cattle and sheep sales, where it is estimated that 50,000 sheep and 1500 cattle pass though its pens each year. There has been an auction mart in Bellingham for over 100 years. Sales are held in January and May, and then between late August and November.

Bellingham's long history as a border town, at the mercy of warring armies and reivers, is reflected in the narrowness of its oldest streets and its fortified church. Most of the grey-stone buildings which flank the wide main street and tiny market place date from the 19th century, including the town hall with its handsome lead clock tower and the Roman Catholic Church (1839) designed by Bonomi. During this period Bellingham was, for a short time, a centre of industrial activity with a large ironworks in the town, and later a railway. The former viaduct of the Border Counties Railway still stands. The line ran between Hexham and Riccarton in Scotland to join the Carlisle to Edinburgh railway, the Waverley line.

The **church of St Cuthbert**, tucked away behind the Black Bull Hotel, dates from the 12th century. It was originally built as a chapel of ease in the enormous parish of Simonburn. The church is one of the few in the country to be given a roof of heavy stone slabs. Legend has it that the Scots burnt down the church so many times it became more economical to have a stone roof. In the churchyard is a coffin called the Lang Pack which, according to legend, was the last resting place of a pedlar who failed to get a band of robbers into Lee Hall a few miles south. The pedlar was allowed to leave his heavy pack in the house though he was refused entry. One of the servants, uneasy about the pack, fired a gun into it and blood began to stain the pack from one of the robbers hidden inside. The alarm was raised and the rest of the band lured to the house – where the majority were shot.

Below the churchyard, on a footpath between the church and river, is St Cuthbert's Well. It is marked by a stone pant erected in Georgian times. The well is said to have healing properties and is used for baptismal water.

Little now remains of the Hareshaw Ironworks at the foot of Hareshaw Dene, bar a few old spoil heaps and the remains of former dams. From here there is an attractive walk through the wooded dene to Hareshaw Linn, a 30-ft (9m) waterfall set in a rocky amphitheatre at the head of the gorge. In **Bellingham Heritage Centre** (run by local volunteers) there are exhibits on the history of the town and its community, including farming, the ironworks and the railway, and everyday life in the North Tyne valley.

BELSAY [Castle Morpeth]

NZ 1078: 5 miles (8km) NW of Ponteland

Belsay consists of a single street built in the form of an Italian-style arcade, and is oddly out of keeping with the surrounding countryside. Close by stands Belsay Hall and its ruined castle, once the home of the Middletons, one of the few pre-Conquest families in England. It is now maintained by English Heritage.

Belsay Hall is a fine Doric-style mansion built between 1810 and 1817 by Sir Charles Monck. It was lived in until 1962.The hall has an elegant interior with much of the original decoration. It is only partly furnished and is mainly used for temporary exhibitions. Opposite stands the shell of the 14th-century castle, with splendid turrets and battlements. It was constructed in 1317 in honey-coloured stone and was the Middleton family's original home. The castle was extended in Jacobean times.

The hall and castle are set in 12 hectares (30 acres) of wonderful landscape gardens including the magical Quarry Gardens. These are planted with evergreens, rare shrubs and rhododendrons. In early spring the woodland is sprinkled with snowdrops and glory of the snow, and later in the year the Magnolia Terrace and Rose Garden come alive with colour.

BELFORD [Berwick upon Tweed]

NU1034: 8 miles (13km) NE of Wooler

A small town of irregular streets and grey-stone houses, Belford was once on the main road between Edinburgh and Scotland. Whilst the traffic may now bypass Belford, the 18th-century coaching inn, the Blue Bell, still dominates the main street. Just behind the inn is the church of St Mary, a fine Norman church which was partly restored by John Dobson in 1828. The church has a tall tower with battlemented pinnacles, loft lancet windows and a Norman chancel arch with zigzag moulding.

Belford Hall was built in the Palladian style and designed by James Paine between 1754 and 1756 for Abraham Dixon. It has been elegantly restored and converted into a number of residential units.

Three miles (5km) west of the town on Belford Moor is **St Cuthbert's Cave**, a natural stone cave on the slopes of Cokenheugh. Now owned by the National Trust, it is said that the saint's body rested here on its journey from Lindisfarne to Durham. A natural pillar supports the massive overhanging rock that forms the front and a stone wall at one time closed the entrance.

BELTINGHAM [Tynedale]

NY7863: 3½ miles (6km)

This pretty hamlet on the banks of the

South Tyne river is fringed by trees and has a tiny green surrounded by stone-roofed cottages. Beltingham's church, dedicated to **St Cuthbert,** stands above the steep-sided ravine of Beltingham Burn with a view over the Tyne valley. Founded as a chapel of ease in the 16th century, the church is reputed tò have Saxon origins. Certainly the yew trees in the churchyard, which are said to be 900 years old, would seem to support this. Two Roman altar stones also stand in the churchyard, one west of the nave and the other beside the gate. The church was restored in the late 19th century but retains many of its original features, including a squint with old iron bars from a former chapel on the site of the 1884 vestry. Some of the south windows are decorated with unusual carvings including a rabbit, fleur-de-lys and a strange human head. Beltingham House, a beautiful Georgian house that once belonged to the Bowes-Lyon family, stands next door to the church.

The wooded gorge of **Allenbanks** was developed as a series of 'wilderness walks' for nearby Ridley Hall (1891) between 1830 and 1860 by Susan Davidson. The hall is now a college but the National Trust owns Allenbanks. Covering nearly 80 hectares (200 acres), the property includes attractive, wooded, terraced walks along the River Allen, an unusual suspension bridge at Plankey Mill, a tarn and the ruins of Staward pele, a medieval tower. Staward pele stands on a grassy platform above a precipitous crag between the Allen and Harsondale burns and is one of the best defended sites in Northumberland. Its 7ft (2m) walls still stand to the height of around 25ft (7.5m).

BERWICK UPON TWEED [Berwick upon Tweed]

NT9953: 14 miles (22km) NE of Coldstream

Berwick, set along the mouth of the River Tweed, is the most northerly town in Northumberland and England. Its strong grey-stone walls and stately Georgian houses crowd the quayside along the banks of the river, famed for its elegant swans and salmon. The Scottish border loops round just north of the town and this proximity meant that Berwick was the focus of hostilities for much of the Border Wars. The town changed hands between the Scots and the English on fourteen occasions before it was given free town status in 1482. Berwick remained a free burgh until the Reform Act of 1885. An interesting bureaucratic anomaly occurred in the 19th century, which meant that technically Berwick remained officially at war with Russia for 110 years. Official documents declaring war on Russia at the start of the Crimean War were in the name of Victoria, Queen of Great Britain, Ireland and Berwick upon Tweed and all British dominions. When the war ended in 1856, the Paris Peace Treaty made no mention of Berwick. The omission was rectified in 1966 when a Russian official made a goodwill visit to the town.

Four bridges cross the Tweed at Berwick. The oldest was built between 1619 and 1634. The Royal Tweed Bridge was built in 1928 to carry Great North Road but has been seded by the modern A1 bridge west of the town. It is, however, the dramatic 28-arched **Royal Border Bridge** carrying the Edinburgh-London railway that dominates the southern approach into Berwick. It stands 38.5 metres (126ft) above the River Tweed. The bridge was built by Robert Stephenson, who demolished most of Berwick Castle to make way for the station on the north side of the bridge. The castle's great hall is now the waiting room, in which a plaque records the decision by Edward I to give the throne of Scotland to John Balliol rather than the more serious rival Robert the Bruce

Berwick Castle was built around 1160, but the earliest surviving sections date from its remodelling under Edward I following his capture of the town in 1296. The castle was abandoned in the late 16th century and became a convenient quarry for many of the town's buildings, including the Barracks. A short stretch of curtain wall and the remains of two towers can still be seen. It was Edward I who began the extensive fortifications of Berwick which still dominate the town. In 1296 a ditch, bank and wooden palisade were built, the palisade being replaced by a stone wall the following year. During the turmoil of the Border Wars, in which the town continually changed hands, the fortifications were repaired by both sides and heightened by the Scots under Robert the Bruce. Traces of these older medieval walls can still be seen around the town.

In 1482 Berwick came back under English control, and was soon considered to be one of the most vulnerable towns in the kingdom. The fall of Calais and the perceived danger of a Scotland ruled by a French regent increased the fear of a Franco-Scottish invasion, which led to the building of the **Elizabethan ramparts** between 1557-70. The last word in military architecture in their time and unique in Britain, they were built to Italian design to withstand artillery bombardment. The substantial earthworks and stone-faced walls are punctuated by a formal pattern of bastions or platforms snaking round the headland. The fortifications were intended to encircle the medieval town, but were never completed and would have left the town seriously undefended if under attack. They were never put to the test but the ramparts can still be followed along the river to a wide, grassy open space between the town and the sea where the various earthworks can clearly be seen.

The 18th-century **town hall** dominates Marygate, the broad main shopping street running down to the River Tweed. The town hall was once a jail and is unique in having a spire where the bell is rung to announce services at the parish church of Holy Trinity, a few streets away. Berwick Town Hall now houses an exhibition on the history of the town with various historical artefacts of local interest. The old town stocks stand alongside.

Holy Trinity Church, standing on Wallace Green, is one of the few churches built during the Commonwealth period after the Civil War. It was built using stone from the castle and contains a wooden gallery. It is said that the church was originally designed to have a tower, but this was omitted at the request of Cromwell, who passed though the town on his way to the Battle of Dunbar. The church contains a beautiful west window made up of twenty-five medallions of 17th-century Dutch or Flemish glass brought from the Duke of Buckingham's chapel at Edgware in Middlesex. The altar screen is late 19th century and by Lutyens. The pulpit is Elizabethan, a relic of the former church. In the south aisle is a monument to Colonel George Fenwick, Governor of Berwick and a friend of Cromwell, who died in 1656. It was at his instigation that the current church was built.

It is thought that Sir John Vanbrugh was the architect responsible for the **barracks.** These were built in 1717 after the first Jacobite uprising. The elegant buildings set around a quadrangle form one of the earliest purpose-built barracks in the country. It was built to accommodate the King's Own Scottish Borderers and now is in the care of English Heritage. The barracks house three museums, one of which chronicles the history of the British army. 'By the Beat of Drum' tells the story of organised army life from Cromwellian times to the present day. The other museums include an exhibition on Berwick and part of the famous Burrell collection from Glasgow. The third museum is a regimental museum dedicated to the Kings Own Scottish Borderers, a Scottish regiment since 1689. This museum contains a fine display of weapons, silver medals and pictures.

The **Wine and Spirit Museum** near the quayside contains some fascinating artefacts used in the brewing and distilling trades. It also includes a recreated Victorian chemist shop.

Haildon Hill to the north-west of Berwick was the site of an English victory for the possession of Berwick in 1333. The Scots under Lord Archibald Douglas were heavily defeated with over 4000 killed by an English army under Edward III. A tall, rugged stone monument on the A6105 commemorates the battle. From here there is a wonderful view of Berwick and the coast, down as far as the Farne Islands and west towards the Cheviots.

BIRTLEY [Tynedale]

NY8778: 10 miles (15km) NE of Hexham

Birtley is set among the rolling green hills of the North Tyne valley. Birtley Hall, built in 1611, contains the remains of a ruined tower that is thought to date from the 16th century. The church of **St Giles** was heavily restored in the 1880s, but still contains a simple chancel arch and heavy round font from the Norman period. Inside the chancel is a small stone square carved with a cross and the letters ORPE. It is thought to date from around AD700. There are also several medieval gravestones built into the porch.

BLANCHLAND [Tynedale]

NY9650: 8 miles (13km) S of Hexham

This is a small moorland village in the Upper Derwent valley with mellow grey-stone houses set snugly round an L-shaped square. At one end stands an imposing 15th-century gatehouse, incorporating the village post office, and

Blanchland

at its other a fine 18th-century hump-back bridge. The present layout of the village dates from the early 18th century, when the trustees of the Crewe Estate built cottages to house lead miners working on the moors above the village. In the centre of the square, opposite the Lord Crewe Arms, is a curious small stone building covering the village water supply. This was erected in 1897 to commemorate Queen Victoria's Diamond Jubilee.

The name Blanchland links the village with its ecclesiastical foundations. The Premonstratensian canons founded an abbey here around 1165. After the Dissolution of the Monasteries in the 16th century, the monks were driven away and the gatehouse and part of the Abbey church are all that now remain.

The **church of St Mary the Virgin** was largely created in 1763, when the tower, choir and north transept of the former abbey church were restored to make a parish church for the people of Blanchland by the Crewe Trustees. It led to the creation of a simple, L-shaped, unpretentious nave-less church, which was further renovated in the 19th century. Surviving from the original building are a massive round pillar dominating the entrance in the east aisle; a font and fragments of 13th-century glass, including the depiction of a monk in a white habit; and a number of medieval gravestones, three of which are of abbots carved with coziers. Outside in the churchyard is a 13th-century cross which would once have stood on the roadside as a shrine for travellers.

Parts of the **Lord Crewe Arms** date back to the 13th century when it formed part of the monastery, but most of the present building is Georgian. In the 18th century it was for a time the home of General Tom Forster, who led the

Post box at Blanchland

unsuccessful Jacobite uprising in 1715. After his capture at Preston, Forster escaped and hid in a priest hole behind the fireplace in the house. The site of the hiding place is still there and so, it is said, is the ghost of his sister Dorothy, who implores visitors to take a message to her brother who fled to France.

From the village there are pleasant walks to **Derwent Reservoir**, which straddles the county boundary between Durham and Northumberland.

BLYTH [Blyth Valley]

NZ3181: 7½ miles (12km) SE of Morpeth

Once a major port, shipbuilding and industrial centre, Blyth was built on the export of coal. It is claimed that one of the first horse-drawn railway lines was developed here in the early 17th century, for the transport of coal from Beside colliery to the riverside. Blyth spreads south along the elongated estuary of the River Blyth and north across the river to where the huge Blyth Power station is sited. The town dates from the 18th century, though few buildings from this period survive, having been swamped by later 19th century and modern development. The lighthouse built in 1788 stands in the centre of the town, but the coal staithes which dominated the harbour area have long since been demolished. Nine 300-kW wind turbines that stand in a row along the East Pier have now transformed the waterfront. From here there are attractive walks south along the beach to Seaton Sluice.

BOLAM [Castle Morpeth]

NZ0982: 8 miles (13km) SW of Morpeth

This hamlet was once a sizeable village with a castle and two hundred houses around a green, but now only Bolam Hall, the vicarage and church of St Andrew remain. The church has a late Saxon tower of rugged grey stone topped with elegant bell lights. The fine Norman interior is greatly enhanced by simple, clear-glass leaded windows. There is a medieval font and a crude effigy of a knight, probably Robert de Reymes (died 1324), the builder of Aydon Castle and neighbouring Shortflatt Tower. From the churchyard on a clear day are views of the Simonside Hills.

Bolam Lake, once part of the Bolam Hall estate, is now a country park. The woodland was landscaped by local architect John Dobson in 1818. He created the lake that has now become an important wintering ground for wildfowl.

BOULMER [Alnwick]

NU2614: 5 miles (8km) W of Alnwick

This small coastal village was once the haunt of smugglers but now only a few single-storey fishermen's cottages remain in what was once a busy fishing village. Set within a natural haven, in a gap through an almost complete band of rock, Boulmer has no harbour. The traditional blue fishing cobles have to be hauled ashore or moored in the water. The main catch is crabs, lobsters and sea salmon. Boulmer was involved in 'rum running', and in some of the oldest houses hiding places were created for casks to be stored. Until fairly recently, casks and forgotten hoards of silk were sometimes dug up on the beach. Just west of the village is the Royal Air Force Warning Station, surrounded by more modern housing.

BOTHAL [Wansbeck]

NZ2386: 2½ miles (4km) NWW of Morpeth

A model village on a side road between Ashington and Morpeth, on a spur between the wooded denes of Brocks Burn and the River Wansbeck, Bothal remains a lovely unspoilt village. The name of the village is derived from the Anglo-Saxon word meaning 'abode'. The village consists of a single street of charming cottages of pale stone, roofed in dark slate with painted pointed gables and lattice windows.

The 13th-century church of **St Andrew** stands in a peaceful wooded churchyard sloping down to Brocks Burn. It has a heavily buttressed bell-cote with three arched openings and a chancel which unusually stands higher than the nave. The 14th-century roof of the nave is made of finely carved oak decorated with angels holding shields. The windows of the south aisle contain fragments of medieval glass. The church contains the alabaster tomb of Ralph, Lord Ogle and his wife Margaret Gascoigne (d.1516), with their two effigies now rather worn but still giving interesting period detail of the clothes of that era.

At the end of the spur above the River Wansbeck stand the ruins of **Bothal Castle**. It was built in 1343 by Robert Bertram and later became the seat of the Ogle family. Little of its central bailey and defensive wall remain, but the fortified gatehouse has been restored and is now used as a guest house. Sir Robert was one of the twelve northern knights who were rewarded by the King for their bravery at the Battle of Neville's Cross in 1346. The gatehouse is adorned with a series of ten shields, which include those of Edward III, the Black Prince, the Percys and the Bertrams. There are also a number of gargoyles and some curious stone figures on the roof. One holds a horn and the other holds a stone in the act of throwing. They were perhaps designed to frighten or confuse the enemy.

BRANXTON [Berwick upon Tweed]

NT8937: 9 miles (14km) NW of Wooler

Branxton is a tiny village lining a side road surrounded by the lush green farmland between the Rivers Tweed and Till. It stands near the site of the Battle of Flodden, marked by a plain granite cross on the A697 Coldstream road. After the battle many of the injured were laid to rest in the **church of St Paul**. Little now remains of the original Norman church that, bar the chancel arch, was rebuilt in 1849. Close to a memorial drinking fountain in the centre of the village is an unusual garden known as the Cement Menagerie. It is populated with giraffes, tigers, farm animals and a motley assortment of famous statesmen, soldiers and countrymen, all modelled in cement!

The **Battle of Flodden** was fought on Branxton Moor on September 9th 1513 between the Scots led by James IV and the English under the command of the Earl of Surrey (Henry VIII was fighting in France.) The Scots were defeated by the skill of the English archers, and in the heat of battle King James was killed together with three of his bishops, thirteen earls and a host of lesser nobility.

BRYNESS [Northumberland]

NT7602: 10 miles (16km) NW of Otterburn

A village set along the A68 and surrounded by Redesdale Forest, Bryness was built as a Forestry Commission village. The adjoining old village includes a few cottages and the church of St Francis of Assisi. Standing just south-west of the village, the little stone-tiled church dates from 1786. In spring its churchyard is filled with wild daffodils. The church contains a remarkable stained-glass window erected in 1903 to commemorate those who died in the construction of Catcleugh Reservoir. It depicts workmen labouring with barrow, pick and shovel on the construction of the reservoir. An engine and truck are beside them and a child is sitting on the ground with her father's dinner wrapped in a handkerchief.

Catcleugh Reservoir was built between 1891 and 1905 to meet the growing water requirements of the people of Tyneside. It was a major undertaking and took nearly fifteen years to complete. Stretching a mile and a half long (2.5km), the reservoir has a capacity of 2345 million gallons (10,670 million litres). A thousand men worked on the dam's construction and a shanty town was served by a narrow gauge railway from West Woodburn that was built to bring construction materials to the site. The navvies' huts were built either side of the River Rede and were known at the time as Newcastle and Gateshead. One of the huts has been restored by the National Park to show what life was like for the people who lived there. The hut is open for educational groups and for special events.

Just south of Bryness is the start of the 12 mile (19km) Forest Drive, an unmetalled toll road which links the A68 with Kielder. The **Three Kings**, which were originally four, are signed off the Forest Drive. The largest stone now lies on the ground, but the other three are still standing and would have once surrounded a cremation cairn dating from the middle of the second millennium BC.

Carter Bar marks the highest point (1370ft above sea level) of the A68 and is the border between England and Scotland. It provides superb views into Scotland and on a fine day these extend to Edinburgh and the Firth of Forth. The current road dates from the end of

Navvies' hut, Catcleugh reservoir, near Bryness

the 18th century and is the only road over the Cheviots into Scotland. This point was previously called Redeswire ('swire' from Old English, meaning 'col' or 'neck') and was the scene of brutal border skirmishes in 1575. The Redeswire Fray is commemorated by the old Border Ballads. During the Border Wars it was one of the meeting places of the Wardens of the Middle Marches, who administered a kind of policing system – sometimes none too fairly. The main duties of March Wardens were to determine the rightful ownership of cattle stolen from one side or other of the border. They also negotiated the return of hostages.

BYWELL [Tynedale]

NZ0461: 5 miles (8km) SE of Corbridge

Picturesquely built around a south-facing promontory above a bend in the River Tyne, the castle, hall, vicarage and two ancient churches are all that remain of a once flourishing town. In medieval times Bywell was famous for its ironwork, primarily bits, buckles and stirrups for the horsemen of the Rede and North Tyne valleys. In 1570 Bywell had fifteen shops, but the town declined during the 18th century as its fishing and ironwork industries dwindled. In the mid-19th century the houses and cottages were removed to create the parkland around Bywell Hall. The villagers were resettled in nearby Stocksfield.

Because of a quirk in the parish boundaries Bywell still has two churches, known locally as Black and White, which stand opposite each other. They are both architectural gems and well worth exploring. **St Andrew's** was founded by the White Canons of Blanchland and is now no longer used for regular worship. It is under the care of the Churches Conservation Trust. St Andrew's is said to have one of the finest Saxon towers in Northumberland, probably dating back to at least 850, with massive stones at its base. The rest of the church is primarily 13th century with 19th-century additions. A number of 13th-century and earlier grave slabs with carved crosses have been set into the walls inside and outside the church. In the chancel is a piece of a Saxon cross shaft set on a carved block that is probably Roman. On the roadside just outside the churchyard stands a medieval market cross shaft topped with an 18th-century finial.

St Peter's Church was founded by the Black Dominican monks in Norman times. The nave of the present church is mainly early Norman and the rest of the building is 13th century. Some parts of the church are Saxon pieces dating from around the early 8th century and are thought to be part of a building that Bishop Egbert of Lindisfarne consecrated in 802. This was later incorporated into the current church. A beautiful church in its own right, St Peter's has a number of interesting features. On a pillar is the carved head of Edward I, who is said to have visited Bywell on one of his expeditions against the Scots. He paid for the rebuilding of those parts of the church damaged by the great fire of 1285.The effect of that fire can still be seen on the north side of the church where the sandstone has been reddened. Halfway up the church tower is a blocked up doorway to which parishioners would have to climb for safety during the Border Raids. Outside the church, on the south wall, is a scratch clock. This is thought to be 12th century and quite rare in the North of England. A rod would have been placed in the hole to cast a shadow on the scratches that indicate the time of the three main religious services. In the churchyard there are a number of interesting 18th-century tombstones engraved with various skeletons and other symbols.

Bywell Castle, now a romantic, roofless ruin, is often called Balliol's Castle, and was, in fact, a gatehouse to a proposed castle that was never completed. The gatehouse was intended to be part of large enclosure and the only other remains are a length of curtain wall running east from the gatehouse The 15th-century tower with its four turrets was built, using mainly Roman stones, for Ralph Neville, the second Earl of Westmorland. It is privately owned and not open to the public.

Bywell Hall is an elegant classical house designed by James Paine in the 18th century for the Fenwick family and altered by Dobson in 1817. It is set in beautifully landscaped gardens. The hall remains in private ownership but the gardens are sometimes open as part of the Northumbria Gardens scheme.

CAMBO [Castle Morpeth]

NZ0285: 10½ miles (17km) W of Morpeth

Built in 1740 as a model village on a ridge overlooking the Wallington Hall estate, Cambo is now owned by the National Trust. The village consists of rows of neat estate cottages and pretty gardens set around a granite drinking fountain in the shape of a dolphin. The village takes its name from 'camhoe', meaning 'a fort or camp on a hill'. The post office occupies a former pele

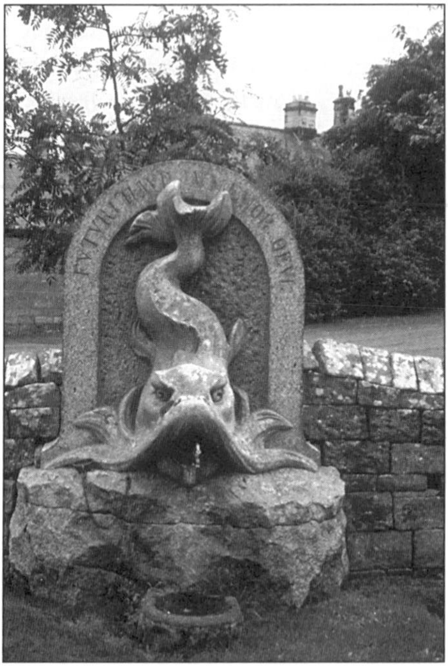

Fountain at Cambo

tower, which is unusual in that it appears to have had three floors. Holy Trinity Church was built in 1842 by Hodgson, the Northumbrian historian and vicar of Hartburn. It has a simple aisle-less nave with whitewashed walls, pine pews and plain glass in most of its windows. Its west tower was added in 1883.

Wallington Hall was built in 1688 for Sir William Blackett out of the proceeds of coal, lead mining and shipping, but the site dates back to medieval times. Embedded in its cellars are the foundations of the pele and medieval castle. The house passed in time to the Trevelyan family, and finally to the National Trust when Sir Charles Trevelyan, a member of Ramsey McDonald's Labour governments of 1924 and 1929/30, left it to the nation.

Eighteen rooms are open to the public, including an Edwardian nursery and kitchen. The house is renowned for its outstanding plasterwork. This was undertaken by Italian stuccatori employed by Sir William Blackett during the remodelling of the building in the 1740s by architect Daniel Garrett. Many of the rooms display part of the hall's stunning porcelain collection and one room is dedicated to a large collection of dolls' houses.

In the central hall there is a magnificent set of eight murals by William Bell Scott, an Edinburgh-born admirer of the Pre-Raphaelites. The murals depict episodes from Northumbrian history from the building of Hadrian's Wall and Bede at work to Grace Darling's rescue of the passengers from the *Forfarshire* and the age of coal and iron. Local worthies of every class found themselves depicted in the murals. In the mural of Hadrian's Wall, Dobson and Grainger's friend and supporter John Clayton, the Town Clerk of Newcastle, is the centurion directing the Ancient Britons building the wall.

Four large griffin heads stand wide-mouthed on the lawn overlooking the road. It is said they were brought back from London in the 18th century as ballast in one of Blackett's coal boats. The gardens were landscaped by Capability Brown, who created a fine parkland of woodland and lakes. The walled garden is particularly special with its pools, terraced walks, herbaceous borders, alpines and Victorian conservatory filled with old and beautiful fuchsias.

The **Wannie Line** is a waymarked 7-mile circular walk that follows the Wannie and Rothbury railway lines which once carried stone, coal and livestock, generating additional revenue for the Wallington estate. The walk starts from the National Trust offices at Scots' Gap.

CAPHEATON [Castle Morpeth]

NZ0380: 11 miles (17km) SW of Morpeth

A model village consisting of attractive terraces of creeper-covered cottages with low, overhanging roofs, Capheaton was rebuilt in the late 18th century. From the village there are attractive views across Capheaton Park towards Sir Edward's Lake with its wooded island. The village is linked to the main road by Silver Lane, so-called after workmen in 1747 found a hoard of Roman coins and plate. They sold some of the coins but gave the rest to the Lord of the Manor, John Swinburne. The collection, which includes a plain sacrificial vessel called a trulla or skillet and the handles of four others decorated with the figures of heathen gods, is now in the British Museum

Robert Trollope, architect of nearby Netherwitton Hall, built Capheaton Hall, the seat of the Swinburne family, in 1668. It has a particularly fine south doorway carved with vines and the figures of a beggar and a knight. The gardens are occasionally open as part of the Northumbria Gardens scheme.

CATTON [Tynedale]

NY8257: 1½ miles (2km) NW of Allendale Town

Catton is built on a steep road descending into the East Allen valley. It is said to have derived its name from its large wild cat population. Just south of the village is the site of the former Allen Mill, a smelt mill constructed between 1845and 1850 under the guidance of Thomas Sopwith, mining engineer of the Beaumont estate. Little remains of the mill except the two horizontal flues that run more than five miles (8km) in total, terminating in stacks on the moors between Allendale Town and West Allendale. It is one of the most extensive flue systems is the country. The flues were designed to produce the intense draught required by the furnace and to facilitate the collection of valuable arsenic deposits. Arsenic was a by-product of lead smelting and was collected by men scrambling along the flues and scraping the arsenic off the walls. The Allen Smelt Mill closed in 1896.

CHATTON [Berwick upon Tweed]

NU0528: 4 miles (6km) E of Wooler

An estate village of mellow stone, Tudor-style houses built around a small village green, Chatton is part of the Duke of Northumberland's estate. The church of Holy Cross was built in 1770, with later Victorian additions including the belfry. There is a memorial in the church to Matthew Culley who became a world-famous agriculturalist at the beginning of the 19th century. He lived in Fowberry Tower, a fine 18th-century stone mansion to the north-west of the village.

CHILLINGHAM [Berwick upon Tweed]

NU0626: 5 miles (8km) SE of Wooler

A peaceful group of estate cottages stand alongside the 12th-century church of St Peter. It has a fine Norman nave and simple bellcote (1753). In the south chapel stands a magnificent alabaster tomb of Sir Ralph (d.1443) and Lady Elizabeth Grey, who served both the Lancastrian and Yorkist kings. Against the tomb chest stand fourteen delicately carved figures of saints and angels.

Chillingham Castle is the ancestral home of the Greys and later the Earls of Tankerville. Originally built as a small pele tower, it was first developed as a fortress in the 14th century. The castle consists of four massive corner towers linked by walls that enclose a large forecourt. The house lay empty for over fifty years, but since the 1980s its interior is being restored. It contains a fine Jacobean ceiling and 17th-century gallery. The grounds were laid out by Sir Jeffrey Wyatville in 1828 and include fine terraces, Italian ornamental gardens and an Elizabethan topiary garden filled with intricately clipped box and yew hedges. The castle is open to the public during the summer months.

Chillingham Castle is best known for its white wild cattle, the purest surviving herd of native British cattle, a breed that has remained unchanged since the Bronze Age. It is thought that when the park wall was built in the 13th century, a wandering herd of cattle was trapped inside the 148-hectare (365-acre) parkland and has remained there ever since. The herd of animals is led by a single 'King' bull that reigns for two or three years until defeated in combat by a younger bull.

Ros Castle An Iron Age hill fort owned by the National Trust stands to the south-east above Chillingham Park. Standing 1000ft (305m) above sea level, its double ramparted earthworks are still clearly visible, but it is the spectacular views of the Cheviots, Farnes and coastal castles that make the climb to the top particularly worthwhile. In 1804 the firing of a beacon here began a celebrated false alarm of a French invasion.

CHOLLERFORD [Tynedale]

NY9170: 4½ miles (7km) NW of Hexham

The village is little more than a small group of buildings clustered around the 18th-century George Inn and bridge. The bridge dates from 1778 and replaced an earlier one that was washed away by the floods in 1771.

Chesters was the 18th-century home of the Clayton family and is set in one of the most beautiful wooded sections of the North Tyne valley. During the 19th century, John Clayton (1792-1890) began the careful excavation of Cilurnum Roman cavalry fort. Clayton was also responsible for acquiring many miles of Hadrian's Wall and several forts, preventing its exploitation as a source of cheap building material and ensuring its survival to the current day.

Now managed by English Heritage, Cilurnum Fort would once have housed 500 cavalrymen. From the 2nd century it was the base for the Second Cavalry Regiment of Asturians (originally raised in Spain), who remained here for 200 years. Chesters was built astride the Wall and its five gateways are still visible, together with the remains of the barrack block, the commandant's house, headquarters and strong room. The highlight is the bathhouse standing on the edge of the fort. It is twenty courses of bricks high and complete with an anteroom, boiler room, warm room and hot bath. Close by are the remains of the bridge that once carried Hadrian's Wall across the North Tyne. The museum contains many of Clayton's finds from many sites along the Wall, including an important collection of sculpture and Roman inscriptions. The museum has barely changed from when it was first founded over 90 years ago and retains its formal glass cases and meticulously handwritten labels.

Hexham Herbs is a specialist herb nursery set in a walled garden with a wildflower meadow and woodland walk. The gardens, open to the public, include fine herbaceous borders, rare plants, old roses, a Roman garden and the national thyme and marjoram collections.

CHOLLERTON [Tynedale]

NY9272: 5 miles (8km) N of Hexham

A tiny hamlet on the bank of the North Tyne, Chollerton consists of little more than a church, the old Borders Railway station and a few cottages. The ruins of **Cocklaw Tower,** a 15th-century pele tower which can be seen on a hillside just south of the hamlet, was probably built with stone from the Roman wall. The church of **St Giles** also incorporates Roman masonry. Four Roman pillars that show the marks of Roman tooling support its south arcade. These may have come from the Roman fort at Chesters. A Roman altar dedicated to Jupiter stands just behind the door and was used as a font. St Giles's dates from Norman times. Later additions include an 18th-century belfry and Victorian spire. A second font sits on a 13th-century carved column and has a Jacobean oak cover. There is similarly richly carved Jacobean panelling in the chancel and the backs of the choir stalls are decorated with foliage, fruit and little birds. In the floor of the sanctuary and the south porch there are a number of fine medieval gravestones. Unusual surviving features are the church stables and the hearse house, with a mounting block in front. These stand by the gate in the churchyard.

COALCLEUGH [Tynedale]

NY8045: 7 miles (11km) SW of Allendale Town

This remote, desolate hamlet once claimed to the highest village in England at 1821ft (555m) above sea level. Little now remains of this one-time lead- and coal-mining settlement at the head of West Allen valley. Most of the houses have gone and all the mine buildings have been demolished, though the shafts and levels still survive along with a scattering of old spoil heaps, on which plants still refuse to grow.

CORBRIDGE [Tynedale]

NY9964: 4 miles (6km) E of Hexham

Corbridge is an ancient town set on a low hill on the north banks of the River Tyne. It is reputed to have replaced Bamburgh as the capital of the Anglo-Saxon kingdom of Northumbria for a short time, following Bamburgh's decline. Corbridge was certainly an important medieval market town at the junction of two ancient highways dating back to Roman times. Today the town has a reputation for its classy shops and pleasant pubs and cafés. Within its grey cobbled streets can be found some fascinating historic buildings, many built using Roman stone taken from the nearby fort of Corstopitum.

Corstopitum was the headquarters and supply base of troops guarding the eastern section of Hadrian's Wall. Founded in the second century AD, the fort and the civilian settlement that grew up around it were occupied to the early 5th century, when Roman rule came to an end in Britain. The fort stood on a crossroads of Dere Street, the Roman road from York and Stanegate running parallel to Hadrian's Wall. The site was excavated in 1906 and is now managed by English Heritage. It contains the best-preserved Roman granaries in Britain. These incorporate an ingenious system of ventilation designed to store grain for long periods of time. The foundations of workshops, temples and houses are all clearly visible. In the visitor centre there is a wealth of Roman material from the whole area, including the Corbridge Lion, a remarkable sculpted fountain head. The fort is linked to the village by a riverside footpath.

The parish church of **St Andrew** is thought to pre-date the death in the town of Ethelred, King of Northumbria in AD796. The base of the tower is Anglo-Saxon and the upper portion 11th century, when the church was repaired following earlier attacks by the Danes. A Roman gateway arch is used to support the tower. The main body of the church dates primarily from the 13th century onwards, including its chancel with three lancet windows at its east end and a priest's door with a finely proportioned trefoil head. There are a number of interesting carved 13th-century gravestones within the church, including one to Lady Alicia de Tynedale with a cross carved in relief and a pair of shears.

In the 14th century a **vicar's pele** was built in the churchyard as protection against the Scots. The tower consists of a substantial vaulted ground floor with a heavy oak door, which was used to stable the vicar's horse. Within the thickness of the wall, built in Roman stone, a stairway climbs to the priest's living quarters above. It is one of the best examples of a small pele tower in Northumberland.

Opposite the church is the attractively cobbled **Market Place,** in which stands a cast-iron market cross bearing the Percy lion. The cross is dated 1814 and was given to the town by the Duke of Northumberland. Previously a market cross had stood for centuries on a Roman altar on this site. This was taken down in 1807 and is now in the Museum of Antiquities. Close by is a pyramid-shaped pant capped by a stone ball which dates from 1815 and which was once fed by a well.

The seven-arched **bridge** over the River Tyne dates from 1674 and is the only one within Tynedale to survive the disastrous floods of 1771. A short distance upstream it is still possible to see the remains of the ten stone piers that carried the original Roman bridge. Just off Aydon Road is Milkwell Lane, was the site of a pottery established in 1840. Here two early 19th-century bottle kilns still stand and are unique in the north of England. **Corbridge Pottery** closed in 1910.

CORNHILL ON TWEED [Berwick upon Tweed]

NT8539: 1 mile (2km) E of Coldstream

An attractive, well-maintained village on the banks of the River Tweed on the English-Scottish border, Cornhill stands opposite the Scottish town of Coldstream. A sandstone bridge joins the two settlements. It was built between 1763 and 1766 by John Smeaton of Eddystone Lighthouse fame. A bronze plaque on the bridge commemorates the poet Robbie Burns crossing the bridge in 1787 and entering England for the first time. The red-tiled toll-house on the Scottish side was once notorious for runaway marriages from England.

Twizell Bridge stands 3 miles (5km) north-east of Cornhill. This narrow bridge over the River Till and above a wooded glen dates from the 15th century. It was the largest single-span arch in Britain until the construction of Causey Arch in County Durham in 1727. The bridge played an important part in the Battle of Flodden in 1530 when the English soldiers led by the Earl of Surrey were allowed to cross the bridge in full sight of the Scottish forces, enabling them to dominate the north flank of James IV's army. On a ridge overlooking the glen is **Twizel Castle,** whose Norman-style ruins in fact date only from the late 18th century. The castle is built on the site of an older fortification which was destroyed in 1496 by James IV during his attack on Northumberland in support of Perkin Warbeck. A small abandoned chapel nearby is said to be where the remains of St Cuthbert rested during his long journey around the region.

CORSENSIDE [Tynedale]

NY8889: 2½ miles (4km) S of Otterburn

Once a sizeable village, it now consists of an isolated house and the church of St Cuthbert set amongst the rolling hills of Redesdale. The name of Corsenside is thought to have derived from Crossensyde, recording the monument which was erected here to commemorate Saint Cuthbert, whose coffin is said to have rested here on its long journey around the North East. The simple grey-roofed church dates from Norman times, but was subsequently altered. It is now rarely used.

CRAMLINGTON [Blyth Valley]

NZ2676: 3½ miles (6km) SW of Blyth

Cramlington is a new town based on an old mining village. It was inaugurated in 1964 and was designed to accommodate industrial and residential development and, as with many new towns, sought to separate cars and pedestrians. Its shopping and leisure centre complex was built in the 1970s adjacent to the old village centre. The old village of mainly terraced housing is set around a small green and includes the parish church of St Nicholas and 18th-century Cramlington Hall.

CRASTER [Alnwick]

NU2519: 6 miles (10km) NE of Alnwick

Craster is an attractive fishing village famous for oak-smoked kippers and filled with small, pretty cottages, many of which are now weekend retreats. The tiny harbour has changed little since it was built in 1906 by the Craster family in memory of a soldier brother killed while fighting in the Tibetan campaign. During the summer, sturdy square-sterned fishing cobles are moored at the harbour, surrounded by nets, ropes and lobster pots. The main catch is sea salmon, lobster and crab. Herrings brought from the West Scottish coast are smoked over white wood chippings at a kippering shed opposite the Jolly Fisherman Inn and are said to be the finest in the world

Behind the village is the great rocky outcrop of Great Whin Sill, from which dolerite stone was quarried until 1939 and shipped from the harbour. The **Arnold Memorial Trail** leads through the quarried wooded crags, illustrating various geological formations. Whin Sill extends to Castle Point, north of the village, where it rises 100ft (30.5m) straight out of the North Sea, forming part of the natural defences of Dunstanburgh Castle.

The grey, craggy ruin of **Dunstanburgh Castle**, captured on canvas by Turner, can be seen on the horizon overlooking the village. Built in the early 14th century by Thomas, Earl of Lancaster and subsequently altered by John of Gaunt, Dunstanburgh was a Lancastrian stronghold for much of the Wars of the Roses, but changed hands five times. In Tudor times the castle fell into decay, and today Dunstanburgh is the largest ruined castle within Northumberland and now in the care of English Heritage. It is reached from Craster by a beautiful coastal footpath.

The castle is entered through John of

Dunstanburgh Castle, near Craster

Gaunt's massive gatehouse built in 1380, which contained the great hall and principal chambers. He built it whilst Lieutenant of the Scottish Marches. From the gateway the curtain wall curves round to the imposing Lilburn Tower, built by Sir John Lilburn when he was Constable of the castle in about 1325. The tower stands three storeys high. Egyndeuch Tower, sometimes called Queen Margaret's Tower after the wife of Henry VI, stands above a rocky gully. It is said that during a siege of the castle Queen Margaret was lowered into the gully below to join a ship waiting in the adjoining cove.

Just inland of the village is **Craster Tower,** home of the Craster family since the 12th century. The tower dates from 1400 and there have been subsequent Georgian wings and Victorian additions.

CRESSWELL [Castle Morpeth]

NZ2993: 7½ miles (12km) NE of Morpeth

This coastal village, close to Druridge Bay, is dominated by its rocky foreshore which stretches far out to sea. Its attractive setting and easy access to Druridge Bay has made Cresswell a popular location for caravan parks. The relatively modern church of **St Bartholomew** is neo-Norman and was built in 1836. It contains some fine stained glass including a memorial to Captain Gilfrid Baker-Cresswell who died of cholera on the march to Alma in 1854 during the Crimean War. **Cresswell Tower**, a rectangular, three-storey fortified dwelling dates from the 14th century and is now roofless.

Druridge Bay is a broad sweep of unspoilt sandy beach stretching 7 miles (11km) along the coast and consisting of 40 hectares (99 acres) of sand dunes and grass hinterland. It was bought by the National Trust in 1972 and is now a nature reserve and country park with a small visitor centre.

DILSTON [Tynedale]

NY9763: 1 mile (2km) SW of Corbridge

The name Dilston means 'Devil's town' or 'the town on Devil's water'. Devil's Water is the name of the stream which runs along a wooded dale into the River Tyne close to Corbridge. Although called a town, Dilston consists only of a mansion, castle ruin, disused tiny 17th-century chapel and narrow 17th-century bridge. Known as the Earl's Bridge, this graceful single-span arch crosses Devil's Water below the ruins of Dilston Castle.

There is no trace of the original mediaeval manor house that was the home of the Divelston family. The tower that formed part of the later Jacobean house was added in the late 15th century. In 1710 James Radcliffe, the third and last Earl of Derwentwater, decided to build a new mansion and demolished all but the tower. As the house neared completion, Derwentwater joined the Jacobite Rebellion of 1715. Following their defeat at Preston, Derwentwater was beheaded on Tower Hill in 1716 for his part in the ill-fated rising. On his death further work on the house was suspended and it was pulled down in 1765 after the estate was confiscated and given to Greenwich Hospital. The tower was left as a roofless ruin. The present Dilston Hall was built in 1835 for John Grey, a famous Northumbrian agriculturalist and father to the social reformer Josephine Bulter.

Further upstream, on the B6306 between Hexham and Slaley, is Linnels Bridge, which crosses Devil's Water in a simple picturesque arch. It was near here that the Battle of Hexham was fought in 1464, the last fling of the Lancastrian cause in the north. After the battle Henry VI is said to have fled for sanctuary to Bywell Castle while his army commander Somerset was captured and beheaded. Linnels Bridge itself was erected in 1698, when the owners of the Linnels were presented by the grand jury of Hexham for having allowed the existing bridge to fall into disrepair. On the parapet of the bridge is an inscription which belonged to an earlier bridge and is written in local dialect, 'GOD PRESARVE WMFOIRA ERENGTON BELLDETE THIS BREGE OF LYME AND STONE 1581.'

DODDINGTON [Berwick upon Tweed]

NT9932: 3 miles (5km) N of Wooler

A compact stone village, Doddington has shrunk in size and importance since medieval times. The village grew up around an ancient spring called Dod Well, which in Victorian times was marked by a simple stone cross. As late as the early 18th century the village held a weekly cattle market and employed local people in the quarry and as hand loom weavers. The enclosure of Doddington Moor in the early 19th century caused the villagers' fortunes to ebb and by 1834 only eight farms remained. Today a few cottages cluster around the 13th-century church of **St Mary and St Michael**, which unusually has its chancel at the west end. This arrangement dates back to a 19th-century restoration by Ignatius Bonomi. The original chancel is now a baptistry, in which sits a massive early Norman font. In the corner of the churchyard is a stone watchtower that was erected in 1826 to prevent grave robbing and body snatching.

In the middle of the village in a farmyard is **Doddington Bastle**. It was built in 1584 for Lord Grey, to protect the villagers against Scottish raids. Now in ruins, the stair turret still stands to a height of around 35ft (10.7m).

Dod Law is a bracken-covered hill overlooking the Till valley and Milfield basin where there are remains of an Iron Age hill fort. Excavations of the area enclosed by the two ramparts have revealed that the site was continually occupied well into the Roman period. Close by are some of the finest examples of cup and ring markings in the county, dating from around 2000BC. There are other prehistoric sites close by at the Ringses and Roughton Linn, both Iron Age hill forts. The latter also contains some particularly fine prehistoric rock art.

DUDDO [Berwick upon Tweed]

NT9342: 7½ miles (12km) SW of Berwick upon Tweed

This tiny hamlet facing the Cheviot Hills derives its name from 'dod' or 'a round hill'. Prominently set on a hilltop close to the village are the **Duddo Standing Stones**. These five standing stones range in height from 5 to 10ft (1.5-3m) and have been weathered into channels on the top. The stones formed part of a 40-ft circle that once enclosed an ancient British burial site. Several burial urns have been found in cairns nearby.

Beside the village stand the remains of **Duddo Tower**, now a tall, shapeless ruin. The Scots destroyed it a few days before the Battle of Flodden. It was restored during the reign of Queen Elizabeth but fell into decay and was further undermined by coal mining.

EDLINGHAM [Alnwick]

NU1109: 5½ miles (9km) SW of Alnwick

Edlingham is a straggling village on the south side of the dramatic curved viaduct (1885) over Edlington Burn. The five-arched viaduct was built to carry the railway between Alnwick and Coldstream, which finally closed in 1964. It is thought that some of the stone to build the viaduct was taken from the nearby ruins of 14th-century **Edlingham Castle**, a fortified manor house, of which only the ruined tower remains. Excavations in the late 1970s revealed that the tower was part of more extensive fortifications, which in the 13th century included a moat, a stone curtain wall and gatehouse.

The **church of St John the Baptist** is largely Norman but is said to have been founded by King Ceolwulf in the 8th century. It has a defensive tower that was added to the west end of the church, covering its original entrance, and can only be entered from inside the church. The priest probably used it as a safe retreat. The church had a particularly fine tunnel-vaulted porch which, though Norman in appearance, is probably 17th century.

EGLINGHAM [Alnwick]

NU1019: 6½ miles (11km) NW of Alnwick

This attractive village of brown stone cottages is set on a slope above the rocky Eglingham Burn. Eglingham's picturesque church of **St Maurice** dates from 1200 and is built on earlier foundations. It was granted by King Ceolwulf of Northumbria to the Lindisfarne monks in 738. The church was sacked by the Scots in 1596 and was rebuilt under General Leslie in the Civil War.

Eglingham Hall is built on the site of a pele tower. The present house is mainly 18th and 19th century but has an unspoilt Jacobean chamber where Oliver Cromwell stayed during the Civil War as a guest of Henry Ogle. Cromwell is said to have quarrelled with his host the following morning! Henry Ogle is also famed for having exposed the notorious Scottish witch finder who was responsible for the execution of fourteen women on Newcastle Town Moor in 1650.

The Ringses is one of the most prominent of a number of late prehistoric settlements to be found on the moors south of the village. It has three great ramparts of earth and stone surrounding the foundations of a few huts, with some others lying just outside the main defences.

ELLINGHAM [Berwick upon Tweed]

NU1725: 5 miles (8km) SW of Seahouses

Ellingham is a small agricultural village built around the restored church of **St Maurice**. Built in 1862, this is a rather unusual church, having a central tower rather than the usual west one. From the churchyard there is an expansive view across the fields towards Preston Tower and the sea. **Ellingham Hall** stands at the end of a quiet lane beyond the village and is the home of the Haggerston family, once supporters of the Stuart cause.

Preston Tower is one of the few defensive structures to survive relatively unaltered from the Border Wars. It is one of the original 78 listed in the survey of 1415 for Henry V. The tower was built around 1392 by Robert Harbottle, Sheriff of Northumberland and Constable of Dunstanburgh during the reign of Henry IV. The original tower had walls 7ft (2m) thick and tunnel-vaulted rooms. After the union with Scotland, half the tower was pulled down and the stone used to build cottages and farm buildings. A new wall was built in 1864 and the tower converted into a clock tower for the modern hall.

Preston Tower is set in attractive grounds and is open to the public during the summer months. It has now been restored to show what it might have looked like in 1400. There is a guardroom and prison on the ground floor, and on the first floor a bedroom and living room furnished with animal skins on the rough bed and reeds on the floor. An exhibition provides a graphic insight into what life would have been like when under constant threat from the reivers who roamed the district, pillaging and stealing cattle, until the late 17th century.

ELSDON [Alnwick]

NY9393: 5 miles (3km) W of Otterburn

This small village built around a large green stands amidst wild and remote moorland. Its name derives from Elles-dene, 'the valley of the waters'. During the Middle Ages, Elsdon was the capital of the Middle Marches, an area stretching from the head of the North Tyne valley to the Cheviots and under the lordship of Redesdale. During this period Elsdon was a busy village at the crossroads of five key trading routes and an important staging post for drovers of Scottish cattle and sheep walking their way to English markets. Salt was also traded and Scottish wool and finished products. Edward I granted a weekly market to Elsdon in 1287 and Lord Redesdale was able to charge market tolls and exact 'a crossing' tax from Scots who came across the border. The creation of the turnpike roads (later A696 and A68) in the 1830s and later the Border railway marked the end of drove roads and packhorse trails and the gradual decline of the village.

Two small grassy mounds overlook Elsdon Burn, which flows through a wooded dene close to the village. Local legend has it that the Danish giant Ella once occupied these mounds. The mounds known as the **Motehills** are all that remain of a 12th-century motte and bailey. The site dates back to Norman

Elsdon

times and was once topped by a palisaded wooden castle and outer buildings. It was built by the de Umfravilles of Prudhoe in 1080. In medieval times the family held the lordship of Redesdale directly from the King. The castle was dismantled in 1157 after Henry II transferred his regional headquarters to Harbottle following the regaining of Northumberland from the Scots.

On the other side of the burn, overlooking the village green is the **church of St Cuthbert**. The prominent 17th-century bellcote is decorated with stone balls and a stubby spire, though most of the church is 14th century, with earlier elements. When the belfry was restored in 1877 three horse skulls were found and it is thought they were placed there either to protect the building from lightning or improve the acoustics. Even more extraordinary was the discovery in 1810 of more than one hundred skeletons beneath the north wall. It is believed that these came from the Battle of Otterburn fought five miles west of Elsdon in 1388 and where the English were defeated by the Scots. Inside, the church has a fine half-barrel-vaulted ceiling and beautiful, clear, leaded-glass windows designed with elaborate patterns. In the north aisle is a Roman burial monument brought from nearby Bremenium (High Rochester). Julia Lucilla erected it to her husband, a surveyor of roadworks.

Next to the church is **Elsdon Tower,** which dates from the turbulent days in the 14th and 15th century. One of the best preserved pele towers in Northumberland, it was altered in the 16th and 19th centuries, including the addition of the pitched roof. The tower was once a rectory but is now a private residence.

Surrounding the village green is a pleasant mix of 18th- and 19th-century farm cottages and former inns, as well as more modern housing. The spacious green would once have been used for herding in animals in times of danger or severe winter. In one corner is a former cattle holding area, or **pinfold** for stray cattle, and a stone slab is all that is left of a former bull baiting ring.

A replica 18th-century gibbet complete with a wooden head stands 2½ miles south of Elsdon village on the Newcastle road. It was originally called **Winter's gibbet** after a murderer who was hanged in Westgate, Newcastle in 1791 for the murder of an old woman, Margaret Crozier. His corpse was hung in chains and displayed on the roadside. Local people once believed that chippings from the gibbet would cure tooth ache if rubbed on the affected spot. Beside the gibbet is the base of a medieval cross base known as Steng Cross.

EMBLETON [Alnwick]

NU2322: 7 miles (11km) NE of Alnwick

This charming village of sturdy stone houses is built on an exposed site above Embleton Bay. The large church of **Holy Trinity** is a late Norman church dating from the 12th century but was much restored in Victorian times. The 13th-century nave arcades are divided by eight-sided pillars supporting pointed arches decorated with dog-tooth decoration. On the northern side of the nave are two amusing 19th-century carved heads, one of a country gentleman and the other of a scholar. The chancel was rebuilt in 1867 and has alternate bands of pink and yellow stone and a fine timber ceiling. In the porch various medieval gravestones have been set into the walls, together with a collection of various architectural fragments. The five windows in the sanctuary are a memorial to Sir George Grey (1799-1882), a Whig who served as Home Secretary for a short time. He was grandfather to Viscount Grey of Falldon, Foreign Secretary when the First World War broke out

Next to the churchyard is the old vicarage, which at one time was a fortified vicar's pele and still retains its rugged tower. The vicarage was largely rebuilt in 1828 by John Dobson in Tudor style.

There is an attractive coastal walk to **Dunstanburgh Castle,** only a mile and half (2km) away (see Craster for description of castle). It goes past fine coastal sand dunes and Gull Crag, a favourite nesting place for fulmars, kittiwakes and guillemots in the spring.

ETAL [Berwick on Tweed]

NT9339: 8 miles (13km) NW of Wooler

This is a charming model village on the east bank of the River Till. A street of attractive, whitewashed, thatched and pantile-roofed cottages leads down to a ford across the river. The river was once bridged at this point and guarded by the 14th-century Etal Castle, but the bridge collapsed during floods in the 16th century. A suspension footbridge provides a pedestrian route over the river.

The now ruined **Etal Castle** began life as a Border tower, but was fortified in the 14th century for Sir Robert de Manners. It has had a turbulent history, frequently besieged by the Scots and was eventually destroyed in 1497 by James IV. A large 18th-century Presbyterian chapel next to the castle has been converted into a visitor centre and contains a superb exhibition on the Border Wars, the Battle of Flodden and the stories of the Ford and Etal estates.

Etal Manor, the 18th-century home of Lord and Lady Joicey, has a fine garden that is open to the public on advertised days. The garden is particularly renowned for its rhododendrons and flowering shrubs which are at their best in May and June, and September and October. In the grounds stands a chapel dedicated to St Mary the Virgin, which was built in 1858 by William Butterfield for Lady Fitzclarence, in memory of her husband who had died in India a few years earlier.

FALSTONE [Tynedale]

NY7287: 8 miles (13km) NW of Bellingham

Sitting below the great Kielder Dam Reservoir at the top of the North Tyne valley is Falstone. Its name is said to have derived from the Anglo-Saxon word meaning 'stronghold'. Part of an Anglo-Saxon cross was found nearby with Roman letters on one side and an Anglo-Saxon inscription on the other. It is now on display in the Museum of Antiquities in Newcastle. At the heart of the village is the old Black Cock Inn and the former village school. The inn was thatched until the end of the last century and its claim to fame is that Lawrence of Arabia once stayed here whilst touring the area on his motorbike. The school is now a tearoom, its kitchen is the former public stable. The tearooms house a Northumberland National Park Information Point. On Whit Sunday each year Northumberland National Park organises an afternoon of traditional folk music, song and dance on the green opposite the tearooms and cast-iron Jubilee drinking fountain. Just south of the village centre is a farmhouse with the date 1604 on its door lintel; this was once an old pele tower and still has a barrel-vaulted ceiling to the living room.

There has been a church on the site of **St Peter's** since the 14th century, and it has been rebuilt several times in its history. The last rebuilding was after faulty heating equipment caused a devastating fire on Boxing Day 1890. In the churchyard are some of the finest 18th-century gravestones in Northumberland, including one of a

Gravestones at Falstone

young girl holding hands with a skeleton and another depicting the dance of death.

The **United Reformed Church** is linked to the late 17th century when Falstone was one of the strongholds of Scottish Presbyterianism in Northumberland. In 1807 the Church of Scotland built the Presbyterian Church, aided by collections taken in Scotland, most notably at Melrose. Over the years much rebuilding has taken place and in 1876 the current tower was added.

High Yarrow Farm is the only reindeer farm in England and is open to the public between April and September. Alongside reindeer there are Cheviot goats, farm animals, fallow deer and birds.

FELTON [Alnwick]

NU1800: 8 miles (13km) S of Alnwick

Felton stands on the north bank of the River Coquet, which is crossed by a 15th-century bridge that once carried the Great North Road, and a modern concrete bridge which now carries traffic through the village. The village has had a turbulent and rebellious past. The English barons met at Felton Park in 1215 to plan the transfer of allegiance from King John to King Alexander of Scotland. In revenge King John burned the town down the following year. The village also supported the Jacobite rebellion in 1715 and Felton Park was used by the Jacobites as a temporary base for northern operations. In 1745 the village switched sides and entertained the Duke of Cumberland on his way to Culloden.

The parish church of **St Michael** stands above the main part of the village and dates from the 13th century although there were later additions. The church has a striking, if rather primitive, bellcote capped by an unfinished church spire, whilst the pitch on the roof of the nave is so flat it appears to be roofless! Inside there is an exceptional tracery window in the south aisle. It is carved from a single stone. In the west window is some golden glass showing the head of St Aidan. This is said to have come from Brinkburn Priory.

To the north of the village is the **Nelson obelisk** which was erected in 1807 by Alexander Davidson, an army clothing contractor who lived at nearby Swarland Hall and who became Nelson's prize-agent after the Battle of the Nile.

FORD [Berwick upon Tweed]

NT9437: 6½ miles (10km) NW of Wooler

Ford is a pretty estate village on the east bank of the River Till, with attractive red-roofed cottages of brown stone. The Marchioness of Waterford rebuilt it in 1859 as a memorial to her husband, who died in a riding accident. A tall column of polished Aberdeen granite carrying the figure of an angel commemorates the Marquis. It stands at one end of an avenue of elegant houses set well back from the road.

Ford Castle sits above the village. It dates from 1338 and was built by Sir William Heron, High Sheriff of Northumberland. It was destroyed several times during the Border Wars, and only three of its four original corner towers are left. Despite being heavily restored by Lady Waterford between 1861 and 65, the castle remains a fine example of a 13th-century square-built fortress. James IV of Scotland spent the night here before his defeat and death at the hands of the English at Flodden Field.

The 13th-century church of St Michael and All Angels stands in the castle grounds and has an interesting bell tower. It was restored by John Dobson in 1853. Between the church and castle, in what is known as Glebe Field, is the portion of a pele tower. It is probably early 16th century and is all that remains after its partial demolition by Lady Waterford, who thought the pele spoiled her view from the castle.

Lady Louisa Waterford, a bridesmaid of Queen Victoria, was an accomplished artist friend of the pre-Raphaelite brotherhood and decorated the old schoolhouse with a series of frescos of biblical scenes, using villagers and children as models. The scenes include Cain and Abel, Moses in the bulrushes, Jacob and Esau. The frescos were painted on paper over a period of twenty-one years and then transferred on to the walls. **Lady Waterford Hall** is open to the public throughout the year.

Heatherslaw Mill, one mile north of Ford on the Etal road, is a 19th-century double acting flour mill powered by a massive undershot waterwheel. The mill still operates when water conditions allow and grinds locally grown wheat into wholemeal flour. The mill is open to the public and there is an exhibition, craft centre and café.

Heatherslaw Light Railway, a delightful 15-inch (38cm) gauge steam-operated railway, runs along the banks of the River Till from Heatherslaw to Etal village. The 3¾-mile (6km) return journey takes 40 minutes.

GREAT TOSSON [Alnwick]

NU0203: 2 miles (3km) SW of Rothbury

The village is picturesquely set above the Coquet and under the steeply rising heights of Tosson burgh. The surroundings hillsides were once said to be the home of mischievous elves called 'Duergars'. Tosson Burgh is the site of an ancient hill fort covering almost two acres (0.8ha). In the centre of this tiny hamlet are the ruins of a 14th-century pele tower, Tosson Tower, which has recently been consolidated. Its four walls and the remains of a staircase can still be seen. Opposite stands a former coaching inn that was once a popular venue for cock fighting, but is now a farm. Just north of the hamlet are the remains of a limekiln (1888) which have recently been restored by the National Park to create an attractive picnic area.

GREENHAUGH [Tynedale]

NY7987: 4 miles (6km) NW of Bellingham

Tarset Burn flows through the conifer plantations of Kielder Forest to the North Tyne river, passing en-route a number of remote farmsteads and the hamlet of Greenhaugh. A natural route for raiders, this valley has several ruined bastle houses including the well-preserved Black Middens and Gatehouse bastles, which have been incorporated into the Reivers Trail. Little now remains of **Tarset Castle**, on a steep-sided promontory above Tarset Burn. It was built in 1267 by John Comyn (Red Comyn) one of the greatest Scottish nobles of that period. This part of the country was part of Scotland as late as 1357, and down to the end of the 15th century Tynedale and Redesdale were regarded as an independent franchise by London. In 1523 Sir Ralph Fenwick held Tarset Castle with a garrison of eighty men. He was driven out by William Charlton of Bellingham and his men, but in 1525 he came back with a group of Tynedale men and Scots and burnt the castle. Much of the stone has been used for other buildings and in 1860 the south-western side of the Castle was destroyed by the construction of the railway cutting of the former Borders Railway.

GREENHEAD [Tynedale]

NY6665: 3¼ miles (5.5km) NWW of Haltwhistle

Sitting in a tight hollow beside Tipalt Burn, Greenhead is built on a natural bridging point. It was a river crossing before Roman times, and used by the Maiden Way and the Roman road Stanegate, and is still used by the modern A69. The slender-spired village church of St Cuthbert was built by John Dobson of Newcastle between 1826 and 28. Inside is a fine east window depicting Christ and the northern saints: Wilfrid, Columba, Aidan and the Venerable Bede.

The **Roman Army Museum** lies half a mile (2km) away from the village. It contains life-size figures displaying the armour, weapons and uniforms of auxiliary and legionary soldiers. The exhibits explore the daily life of a Roman solider, his training, pay and off-duty pastimes. Close by are the few visible remains of the Roman fort Carvoran, known as Magna by the Romans. It was built to guard the crossing of the Tipalt and the junction of Stanegate with the Maiden Way from Alston.

Opposite the Roman Army Museum is **Walltown Quarry,** opened in 1871. It employed 40 men and produced about 100 tons of whinstone a week, which was used mainly for road making. The quarry destroyed an impressive section of Hadrian's Wall and only closed in the early 1970s, leaving an ugly scar on the landscape. A major reclamation scheme has subsequently been undertaken by the National Park and the area infilled and landscaped with trees and shrubs and the quarry pond made into a lake. The quarry is now a recreation site and a number of themed trails have been developed. The Quarry Trail looks at the industrial history of the site and a geology trail 'The Hard Rock Trail' explains the history of the formation of the rocks in the quarry through a number of sculptures.

GILSLAND [Tynedale]

NY6366: 5 miles (8km) W of Haltwhistle

Gilsland is on the border between Cumbria and Northumberland and surrounded by attractive countryside. It lies close to the dramatic Irthing Gorge and Carmel Linn waterfall, and Hadrian's Wall runs through the centre of the village. The development of Gilsland owes much to tourism, with the opening of the first Spa Hotel in the

1740s and the construction of the Newcastle-Carlisle railway in the mid-19th century. In its heyday, Victorian Gilsland was a popular weekend retreat, but the decline in the fashion for taking the waters and the advent of the motor car saw its popularity fade. The village still attracts walkers and the opening of the Hadrian's Wall National Trail, with a new footbridge across the river linking the village to the Roman fort at Birdoswald, is likely to bring more visitors to the area.

Gilsland lies on the red rock fault where limestone changes to red sandstone. It has resulted in some important geological features including the Irthing Gorge and an enormous number of springs, over 600 in one part of the village alone. Gilsland's waters have been famous since ancient times. The first Spa Hotel was built in 1740 and it became a highly popular watering place, appearing in guidebooks alongside Bath and Harrogate. The spa well still exists in the grounds of the Spa Hotel. With the decline in interest in spas, the Spa Hotel was taken over by the North Eastern Co-operative Society, who used it as a miners' convalescent home. It is now a hotel.

Gilsland and the surrounding area contain a number of important Roman remains. The section between Gilsland and Willowford Bridge is regarded as one of the most instructive miles on the Wall as it illustrates a number of key features, including the foundations of the broad wall, a milecastle and turret. The milecastle at Poltross Burn, known locally as the King's Stables (a local legend links it to King Arthur), is a particularly fine example and has been used to calculate the probable height of the Wall. The section from Gilsland School to Willowford Bridge demonstrates where the original plan to build a broad wall 10 Roman feet wide was altered and a narrower wall built on the original broader foundations. Close to Willowford Farm are the remains of Willowford Bridge abutment, although this is now some distance from the river, which has moved west since Roman times. **Birdoswald,** the Roman fort of Camboglanna, lies one mile (1.5km) west of the village, standing on an escarpment overlooking the River Irthing. The fort has been partly excavated and a visitor centre contains an exhibition on the history of the site and a collection of finds.

Gilsland has quite strong associations with the poet and novelist **Sir Walter Scott** (1771-1832). Scott stayed at Wardrew House as a young man and met his future wife, Mademoiselle Charlotte Charpentier, the daughter of a French émigré, there. He proposed to her at a large boulder near the Irthing river, which subsequently became known as the popping stone. It is said to be half its original size, having been chipped away by young ladies who placed small pieces under their pillows as a charm to encourage young men to 'pop the question'. Scott later immortalised Gilsland in his novel *Guy Mannering*.

GLANTON [Alnwick]

NU0714: 10 miles (16km) W of Alnwick

Glanton is a quiet village set on the junction of five roads. Its elevated position commands extensive views across the Breamish valley and the broad green plain of the Vale of Whittingham. Glanton is a good example of a rural village rebuilt following the 1763 completion of the Northumberland section of the London to Edinburgh road through Newcastle to Kelso. It contains a number of attractive 18th-century grey-stone houses.

In 1648, during the Civil War, Royalist troops camping overnight in Glanton found themselves prisoners. Parliamentary troops under the command of Colonel Sanderson, hearing of their movements, came under the cover of darkness and surrounded the unguarded camp, capturing one hundred and eighty soldiers.

The **World Bird Research Station** opened here in 1930 for the study of wild birds in the Border region. It organises the annual recording of dawn and dusk choruses throughout the British Isles. The Bird Field Study Museum is open in the summer on advertised days and contains exhibits on birds of Northumberland and further afield.

GREAT SWINBURNE [Tynedale]

NY9375: 7 miles (11km) N of Hexham

This settlement takes its name from Swin Burn, which flows through a wooded ravine below the village of Great Swinburne. Most of the cottages once housed workers from the estate of **Swinburne Castle**. Of the original castle nothing exists, and there is little of the 18th-century house which replaced it, although the 17th-century manor house still survives. The castle is still privately owned by the Swinburne family – who took part in the 1715 Jacobite rebellion.

Half a mile south of the village is the largest standing stone in the county. A red sandstone monolith over 3 metres (10ft) high, it has incised grooves running down the sides and is decorated by a series of 'cup and ring' markings.

GUNNERTON [Tynedale]

NY9075: 7 miles (11km) NNW of Hexham

This agricultural village stands on both banks of Gunnerton Burn, which flows down to the North Tyne river. The church of **St Christopher** was built in 1900 to a prize-winning design by a young architect named Hawes. He later took holy orders and became a hermit on Cat Island in the Bahamas. Half a mile (1km) north of the village, set in private woodland on Money Hill, are the remains of a medieval motte and bailey defensive site.

GUYZANE [Alnwick]

NU2103: 4 miles (6km) W of Amble

Guyzane derives its name from Guines, a village near Calais, and is one of the few Norman place names used in the county. The village faces south above a wooded bank on a loop of the River Coquet and consists of a single street of 18th-century cottages that were remodelled in Victorian times.

South of the village, a long, stone bridge crosses the river. Above it stands a former mill, now known as the Dye House. This was built in 1775 as a tin and iron foundry, before being converted into a woollen mill in 1791. It was later used in the manufacture of alumina, to make the white pigment from which the building derives its current name. As part of its conversion into a woollen mill, a weir was constructed by John Smeaton, the famous engineer, to turn a mill-wheel. The weir almost destroyed the Coquet as a salmon river until a hundred years later, when a local naturalist was able to persuade the Duke of Northumberland to build a salmon ladder.

The remains of **Brainhaugh Priory** stand in a walled 18th-century graveyard below the bridge. Little now remains of the original Norman chapel which Richard Tyson gave to Alnwick Abbey and which may have been used by the small Premonstratensian nunnery of 'gysnes'. Up until the 18th century it is said that marriages were performed in the roofless building and services held under a neighbouring thorn tree.

Guyzance Hall is famous for its rose garden and herbaceous borders, which are open to the public on advertised days.

HALTWHISTLE [Tynedale]

NY6163: 14½ miles (23km) W of Hexham

Haltwhistle is a busy, unpretentious small market town, where coal mining and quarrying have given way to light industry. Its name has nothing to do with trains, despite being on the site of the former junction with the South Tyne branch line to Alston. Haltwhistle probably means 'a junction of streams by a hill'. Leading from the small rectangular market square are a number of stone and cobbled alleyways lined with a grey-stone buildings. There are some elegant shopfronts on the main street. The whitewashed Red Lion Hotel incorporates a pele tower, a relic from a turbulent past when townspeople and animals would shelter from marauding cattle thieves. There are also a number of other pele towers and strong houses within the centre of Haltwhistle, but these have been so substantially altered as to be now unrecognisable.

Holy Cross Parish Church is claimed to have been founded by William the Lyon, King Of Scotland in 1178. (At one time the Scottish kingdom included most of Cumbria and Northumberland so the border was much further south than at present.) The church dates from 1200 and has a simple exterior and spacious interior with a fine, painted chancel roof thought to be by Kempe and some stained glass from the William Morris factory.

On the outskirts of the town is Haltwhistle Burn and an attractive footpath follows the burn across Stanegate, the former Roman supply road to Vallum. It reaches **Hadrian's Wall** near the Cawfields picnic site and the site of the Roman fort Aesica at Great Chesters.

Close to Haltwhistle are a number of impressive halls including **Bellister Castle,** a Victorian building which, although owned by the National Trust, is not open to the public. The current castle stands on the site of a pele tower. **Blenkinsopp Hall** is a privately owned 19th-century house in attractive gardens that are open to the public on advertised days. **Featherstone Castle** was used in the Second World War as a

POW camp for German officers, but is now a private dwelling. Parts of the house date from the 14th century, when it was used as a medieval tower house. There were Jacobean additions and substantial alterations in the 19th century, when it was Gothicised to create a romantic dwelling.

HARBOTTLE [Alnwick]

NT9304: 8 miles (13km) NW of Rothbury

A pretty village of pale sandstone cottages nestling beneath the ruins of a castle. The name Harbottle derives from Here-bothy, 'the bothy or station of an army'. It is an ideal site for a fortress, designed to command the routes through Upper Coquetdale, and stands on high ground surrounded by the River Coquet on three sides, at a point in the river known locally as the Devil's Elbow.

The first timber castle was built by Robert de Umfraville, one of William the Conqueror's knights. Later Henry II ordered the de Umfravilles to replace the building with stone following the transference of Northumberland from Scotland to England in 1159. These fortifications were substantial and were able to resist Scottish attack in 1219, but were captured by Robert the Bruce in 1319 after Bannockburn. Harbottle Castle was later returned to English hands and was repaired under Edward III. Here, on October 15th in 1511, Henry VIII's sister Margaret gave birth to a daughter, afterwards grandmother of James VI of Scotland and I of England.

In 1545 the castle was handed over to Henry VIII in exchange for other property elsewhere and the keep was largely rebuilt using stone from the monasteries at Holystone and Brinkburn. In the

Harbottle Castle

troubled years of the Border Wars and raiding, Harbottle became the last outpost on the English side of the border. It was later to become the stronghold of the Lords of Redesdale, who were said to have felt safer here than amongst their own wild dalesmen. It is surrounded within a radius of 6 miles (10km) by no fewer than sixteen pele towers.

By the early years of the 17th century, Harbottle Castle was in ruins and its stone was gradually plundered for walls and local cottages, including the shooting lodge (1829). This is also known as Harbottle Castle and was built by Dobson at the east end of the village. It is now a private house with a craft centre. However, substantial fragments of the original castle's curtain wall remain – parts of the keep and the grass-covered foundations of the eastern gatehouse.

The Drake Stone stands west of the village on Harbottle Crags Nature Reserve and is linked to it by a footpath. A massive block of reddish grey fell sandstone close to a small lake, the stone is said to have provided the setting for various primitive rites.

HARTBURN [Castle Morpeth]

NZ0986: 11 miles (7km) W of Morpeth

A sheltered village set above the wooded ravine of Hart Burn, it contains a delightfully unspoilt 13th-century church. **St Andrew's** is associated with the Knights Templars, whose symbol, the Maltese cross and dagger, can be seen inside the entrance of the ornate south doorway. The most striking feature of the church, quite common in Northumbrian churches, is that the chancel inclines sharply away at an angle from its nave. Traditionally this is meant to represent the droop of Christ's head on the cross. It is thought that the church's squat Norman tower may have once been free-standing and provided the living quarters for the priest, who would have climbed up to these using a rope or ladder. It was not until the middle of the 13th century that a stone staircase was added.

A few years ago a number of skeletons were found in the walls of the tower. These have been dated from between 966 to 1166. A charter of King John in 1207 shows that at that time the church belonged to the monks of Tynemouth Abbey, but later it seems to have been taken over by monks from St Albans called north to rescue the declining monasteries.

Inside the church is a memorial to John Hodgson, the Northumbrian historian who was vicar in Hartburn between 1833-45. Noting holes which belonged to a timber bridge across Hart Burn, Hodgson was able to trace the line of the **Devil's Causeway,** a Roman road which crossed Wansbeck river near Hartburn and headed north-east, linking Corbridge and the Roman road of Dere Street to Berwick and the mouth of the Tweed.

The medieval-looking pele tower on the left on entering the village is, in fact, an 18th-century structure built by the parishioners under the direction of the then vicar, Dr Sharp (1749-92). Its ground floor was used as the parish stables and the upper floor housed the schoolmaster.

Marlish Farm (1 mile (2km) south-west) is a working farm open to the public, with a varied collection of farm animals including goats, donkeys and pigs, many of which are quite tame and happy to be stroked. A number of old tractors have been left around the farm for children to play on and there are indoor and outdoor picnic facilities.

HAYDON BRIDGE [Tynedale]

NY8464: 6 miles (10km) W of Hexham

Snug, grey-stone houses cluster either side of the South Tyne, in a village which, as its name suggests, developed as a major crossing point on the river. During medieval times the bridge was used by warring Scottish and English armies, and was often barred and chained against Scottish raiders. There are currently two bridges crossing the river here; a modern concrete structure carrying the A69 and a stone bridge of 1815 which replaced a whole series of earlier bridges on this site that had been damaged by flooding.

On a hillside above the current village is the site of **Haydon Old Church** and the site of the medieval village. The church is said to have been built on the site where St Cuthbert's body rested on its way around Northumbria. It dates from the 12th century and its western side was demolished to provide stone for the new St Cuthbert's, with its lead-covered spire. This was built in 1796 and stands in the centre of the village on the north bank of the river. The chancel and chapel of the Old Church were restored in 1882. Inside is a font made from a re-cut Roman altar and a 14th-century chantry chapel with a wonderful eastern window.

Haydon Bridge is a former spa and the original spring can be seen on the eastern approach to the village, where a flight of five steps lead down to a stone basin beside the river into which fresh water trickles.

HEDDON ON THE WALL [Castle Morpeth]

NZ1366: 4 miles (7km) SW of Prudhoe

Heddon contains the first clearly visible section of **Hadrian's Wall** when travelling west from Newcastle. It was built to the original broad gauge of 10 Roman feet wide. The visible masonry dates mainly from the 3rd and 4th centuries and the stones would once have been set in puddled clay. On the western side of the remains is a medieval limekiln carefully built into the ruins. The village itself stands on the site of the milecastle where a hoard of 5000 silver coins dating from AD244-75 was found in 1879.

On a little hill in the centre of the village stands the ancient parish church of **St Andrew's,** dating from Anglo-Saxon and Norman times. Inside its 12th-century chancel is fine stone vaulting and on a windowsill lies a Saxon cross head. The crude stone font is Norman and near it stands an old oak chest bound with simple ironwork.

A terrace of brownish grey cottages in the village has an interesting history. Known as 'Frenchman's Row', they were built in 1796 for local miners, but before they were complete they were allocated to French royalist refugees who had fled the country during the

Revolution, as an act of charity. The big square sundial on the front of one was erected as a thank-offering when they returned to France in 1802.

HEPPLE [Alnwick]

NT9800: 5 miles (8km) W of Rothbury

A hamlet of pretty grey cottages, Hepple lies on the slopes of Wreghill Pike in Upper Coquetdale. The community has had a turbulent past having been twice destroyed, once by the Scots in 1412 when the chapel on Kirk Hill was sacked (marked by a stone cross) and in 1665 when the inhabitants died from plague.

The 19th-century **Christ Church** contains a number of fragments of the medieval chapel, including the primitive Norman font with carved figures – of which only a bearded man is visible. This contrasts with the brightly painted interior. East of the church are the ruins of 14th-century Hepple Tower. Standing in a farmyard beside the main road, its western walls are still well preserved, standing nearly 30ft (9m) high.

Witchy Neuk Camp, on the summit of Swindon Hill, is a well preserved Iron Age hill fort giving magnificent views of the Coquet valley. It was excavated in 1936 and seems to have been defended by a single rampart and ditch. Finds including a quern for grinding corn, iron slag and fragments of 3rd-century Rhenish glass suggest continuous or later occupation of the site.

Harehaugh Camp is another nearby Iron Age hill fort. Set on a spur overlooking the valleys of the Coquet and Grasslees, with superb views of the surrounding area, it consists of three massive ramparts and deep ditches and encloses a large area of land. In more recent times the area of flat green land on the bend of the river below Harehaugh was a favourite meeting place for cock fighting and racing.

HEXHAM [Tynedale]

NY9364: 20 miles (32km) W of Newcastle

Now the administrative centre for Tynedale District, this picturesque old market town dates back to Saxon times, when the abbey was founded. Hexham developed as a crossing point on the River Tyne and for centuries passengers were ferried over the river by boat. The best view of Hexham is from the Tyne Bridge, looking up to the ridge where the town's main buildings stand above the river, the skyline dominated by the great square tower of its abbey. The current bridge was built in 1793 and replaced two previous ones erected in 1770 and 1780 which were damaged in floods.

St Wilfrid built **Hexham Abbey** in 674 and it is dedicated to St Andrew. Of the original church only the crypt and apse still survive under the current choir. One of the greatest treasures from this period is St Wilfrid's chair, once used as a frith or sanctuary stool. It is at least 1300 years old and reputed to be the coronation seat of the kings of Northumbria. Halfdene the Dane sacked the abbey in 876, along with much of what is now Tyneside. The church was re-founded by the Augustinian canons in the 12th century, when the priory church was built. Much of the current building uses Roman stone, probably taken from Corbridge, including a number of inscribed stones, many of which are on display. Of particular interest is a Roman tombstone at the foot of the night stairs that linked the monastery dormitory to the abbey. It is dedicated to a twenty-five-year-old standard-bearer called Flavinus, c.AD80-98.

The nave dates only from 1908 and replaced one badly damaged by the Scots in the late 13th century. The north and south transepts, built in the 13th century, consist of a wonderful series of carved arcades and arches rising upwards to the 15th-century wooden ceiling, creating a wonderful sense of light and space. The southern transept contains the night stairs and a special doorway called a slype that connected the graveyard with the cloister. The chancel is crowned with a ceiling of beautifully carved 15th-century floral bosses. Similarly, the choir stalls are mostly 15th century, including some surviving misericords carved with roses, shields and grotesque heads. The chancel screen is perhaps one of the finest in England, with much of its original red, green and gold decoration. Thomas Smithson, Prior, erected it from 1491 to1521. It contains paintings of the Annunciation and the Visitation and sixteen portraits of the bishops of Hexham and Lindisfarne. Another wonderful 15th-century screen is that on the north side of the sanctuary, which contains medieval paintings of the seven Hexham bishops who became saints – including Wilfrid and Cuthbert.

The abbey contains some wonderful examples of medieval gravestones, including the head of the grave of Bishop Acca, the patron of Bede, who died in 740. There is also a memorial to King Elfwald of Northumbria, murdered in 788. The abbey also has a copy of the Breeches Bible dating from 1612 (so called because in Genesis 3:7 it has been translated as Adam and Eve making breeches instead of 'clothing themselves'). Only the priory gate and parts of the chapter house remain from the once extensive monastic buildings that supported the abbey prior to the Dissolution of the Monasteries. Part of the site is now an attractively landscaped park known as the Priory Grounds.

The Priory overlooks the **Market Place**, an attractive square from which various narrow streets lined with Georgian buildings begin. In the middle is a long shelter or shambles erected in 1766 where a market is held. This was the scene of the famous Hexham riot of 1761, when a crowd of 5000 assembled to object to the conscription that was introduced to raise troops to fight the war against Napoleon. As the Riot Act was read to the protestors, the soldiers guarding the magistrates panicked and opened fire, killing 51 people and injuring 300. For years afterwards the North Yorks Militia were known as the Hexham Butchers.

Opposite the abbey is the **Moot Hall**, a vast gatehouse to the castle built in 1335. The gatehouse housed the courthouse and bailiffs of the Archbishop of York, who was the Lord of the Liberty and Regality of Hexham. A stone passageway leads from the gatehouse to what was once a fortified manor house and served as the Archbishop's prison. Built between 1330 and 1332, the walls are an amazing 11ft thick and constructed using Roman stone. The old gaol was in use until 1824. It now houses the **Border History Museum** and contains displays on life during the Border Wars when blackmail, feuding, and cattle and sheep stealing dominated the lives of ordinary people.

Tyne Green Riverside Country Park extends 19 hectares (47 acres) along the banks of the River Tyne and there is an attractive trail between Hexham Bridge and Watersmeet, where the North Tyne and South Tyne rivers meet.

South of the town is **Hexham Racecourse** and close by is Queen's Cave. Here, after the **Battle of Hexham** in 1464, Queen Margaret and her infant son hid. The battle was the final victory of the Yorkists over the Lancastrians in the Wars of the Roses, ending the four-year battle of Henry VI and Edward IV. The Lancastrian leader Henry Beaufort, Duke of Somerset was beheaded in the town's market place. The Queen's Cave by Dipton Burn is cut into a soft sandstone cliff. It is said the Queen sought refuge here for two nights before escaping to Scotland

HIGH ROCHESTER [Tynedale]

NY8398: 5 miles (8km) NW of Otterburn

The hamlet of High Rochester is built inside the ruins of a Roman fort and is a rare example of a Roman site being used by successive generations without its origins being totally obliterated. Its Roman name was **Bremenium** ('the place of the roaring stream') and the fort was built around AD80, probably by Agricola. For two hundred years it was the most northerly occupied fort in the Roman Empire. It would have housed a unit of 1000 cavalry, and during its occupation was garrisoned by units from Spain, France, Belgium and Yugoslavia. By the mid-19th century the fort walls, gateways and internal buildings had been dismantled to provide stone for other cottages and field walls. Only the outer defences, grass-covered ramparts, part of the turret in the south wall and the well-preserved western gateway now survive. Other stone blocks from the walls and towers of the fortress can easily be picked out and the former school house's entrance porch is made entirely of Roman stone.

Excavations of Bremenium have revealed a sunken strongroom in the headquarters of the building (protected by a stone slab which ran on iron wheels), two granaries and many altars and inscribed stones. Some of the latter are on display in Alnwick Castle. The fort is close to the site of the Roman Dere Street. Between High Rochester and Chew Green there are nine temporary Roman camps and one of the best preserved lies 400 metres west-north-west of High Rochester. South-east of the hamlet, near Petty Knowes, is the remains of a Roman cemetery. It contains at least ninety graves, of which the most prominent is the lower course of a circular, stone Roman tomb. Two of the stones are carved with the worn relief of pine cones and the horned head of a deer, Roman symbols associated with death.

The hamlet also contains two 16th-century bastles. The more complete is simply known as The Bastle. This was an area at the heart of the Borders skirmishes and a ferocious raid by Scottish reivers the Elliots of Liddesdale in 1583 left the village to waste for five years.

HOLY ISLAND [Berwick upon Tweed]

NU1241: 11 miles (17km) SE of Berwick upon Tweed

Lindisfarne Castle, dramatically set on a craggy outcrop of whin sill, dominates the view to Holy Island from the mainland. The island of Holy Island is accessed at low tide by a three-mile causeway that was built in the 1950s, which for five and a half hours each day is covered by water. The ancient pilgrim crossing from Beal to Holy Island is still visible, marked by poles across the sand flats.

There is just one village on Holy Island, or Lindisfarne as it was known in medieval times. Though many islanders are involved with tourism, some still fish for crab and lobster from the little harbour. Along the harbour foreshore are the upturned wooden hulls of fishing boats which were once used to catch herring but have now been converted into fishermen's huts. In the centre of the village square is a market cross erected in 1828 on a medieval socket. The main street of Marygate is lined with pleasant houses, one of which is **The Museum of Island Life.** Based in an 18th-century fisherman's small cottage, the museum depicts how families worked and lived on the island.

Lindisfarne Priory is one of the most important centres of early Christianity in England. The original episcopal see and monastery were founded by St Aidan in 635. St Aidan came from Iona in the Scottish Highlands at the request of the Northumbrian King Oswald. It was originally a simple collection of huts within a defensive enclosure, but from here the monks went out to preach first to neighbouring villages and then further afield. Aidan prepared twelve bishops to continue his work and on his death he was succeeded by St Finian, who continued the expansion of Christianity.

In 664 **St Cuthbert** came to Holy Island and was to become the most famous of the Lindisfarne bishops, due in part to his powers of oratory and strong asceticism. In 676 he retired to a small cell in the neighbouring Farne Islands, but later unwillingly accepted the bishopric of Hexham in 684. In the following year he became Bishop of Lindisfarne. Soon afterwards he returned to the Farne Islands, where he died in 687. His body was taken back to Lindisfarne to be buried. Eleven years later it was decided to move his body to a more honoured place within the church and it was found that it had not decayed. Cuthbert's body was placed in new vestments and a new wooden coffin decorated with elaborate carvings.

St Cuthbert's remains became an important sacred relic. When the monks fled Holy Island to avoid attack by the Danes in 875, they took Cuthbert's body with them. For the next eight years the monks carried his coffin around the North of England, rarely settling in one place until they finally settled at Chester-le-Street in 883. Fear of further Danish attack in 995 led the monks, instructed by divine revelation, to take St Cuthbert to Dunholm, the site of the present cathedral city of Durham.

Most of work developing the priory occurred after Cuthbert, under his successor St Wilfrid. His incumbency coincided with what has been described as Northumbria's golden age, where there was a flowering of the arts and scholarship. One of the greatest masterpieces produced in this period was the *Lindisfarne Gospels,* now in the British Museum. This beautifully illuminated manuscript is thought to have been produced by Eadfrith, later Bishop of Lindisfarne.

In AD793 Lindisfarne Priory was sacked by the Vikings and most of the monks were slain. Despite this the priory survived and continued until 875, when fear of a second major attack caused the flight of the monks. Lindisfarne was re-founded in 1080 as a dependent priory of Durham and it is the ruins of this later monastery that can be seen today.

The Priory has been in ruins since the Dissolution of the Monasteries and is now in the care of English Heritage. One of the most striking features is the rainbow arch over the nave, which still links the transepts carved with zigzag ornamentation. Close to the priory, on a tiny island, is the site of an alleged 7th-century cell used by St Cuthbert. It is cut off at high tide and the low remains visible on the island today are from a medieval chapel.

The **Lindisfarne Priory Museum** has an excellent exhibition on the life of the early monks. It has many carved stones from the Anglo-Saxon and Viking periods, including the so-called funerary 'pillow stones'. There is also a famous 9th-century stone carved with a band of marauding Viking warriors on one side and a symbolic representation of the Day of Judgement on the other, depicting the terror of the monks.

St Mary's Parish Church was thought to have been built between 1120 and 1145, though other than some masonry in the western corner it predominately dates from the 13th century. Its long chancel is 13th century and three eastern arches in the north arcade are decorated in alternate use of red and white stones – the only such examples in Northumberland. In the wall of the chancel is a medieval tombstone carved with a cross and sword. The north porch was built in the early 19th century and designed as a mortuary for the victims of shipwrecks.

Lindisfarne Castle sits romantically on top of rocky Bexlome Crag. It was built as part of coastal defences in 1550, during the reign of Henry VIII, using the stone from the priory. The fort continued to be used as a garrison until 1819 and was then used by the coastguards. In 1903 the castle was bought by Edward Hudson (founder of *Country Life* magazine) and transferred into a magnificent private house by Sir Edwin Lutyens. Lutyens left the basic fabric of the castle alone, including the two steeply-pointed tunnel vaults in the dining room and Ship room, but created various passages hewn into the rock, large vaulted chambers and a long gallery linking the upstairs bedrooms. The castle and its tiny walled garden designed by Gertrude Jekyll were given to the National Trust in 1944 and are now open to the public. The castle contains a fine collection of mostly oak, early 17th-century furniture of English and Flemish origin.

Lindisfarne National Nature Reserve extends 3240 hectares (8000 acres) from Goswick Sands in the north to the southern part of Budle Bay to the south, with Holy Island at its centre. The habitats of sand, mudflats, sand dunes and saltmarsh provide an important overwintering ground for wildfowl and a breeding ground for birds such as the little tern, ringed plover, brent-goose and other waders. There is also a rich collection of marsh plants including sea aster, thrift and scurvy.

There are splendid walks all over the island, which is 3½ miles (6km) long and approximately 1 mile (1.5km) across at its widest point. From the south end of the island there are views to the beacon obelisks on the main shore which were built between 1820 and 1840 for Trinity House by John Dobson. They were built in 1860 to guide shipping carrying lime and coal to and from Holy Island. Holy Island is also famous for its Lindisfarne mead produced by **St Aidan's Winery** from honey. The winery is open to the public.

HOLYSTONE [Alnwick]

NT9502: 6½ miles (11km) W of Rothbury

Just south of the banks of the Coquet river is Holystone, a secluded hamlet of closely packed cottages which until the late 19th century were mostly thatched. It is here that St Paulinus is said to have baptised 3000 Northumbrians during Easter week AD627. The site is marked by **Lady's Well**, a pool fed by a clear spring standing in a grove of trees. Owned by the National Trust, Lady's Well is reached by a footpath beyond the late 17th-century Salmon Inn.

A highly evocative and atmospheric place, an inscribed stone cross stands in the centre of the pool and is reflected in the water. At one end of the pool is a statue dedicated to St Paulinus which was brought from Alnwick Castle in 1788. No one is sure of the site's origins. Some believe it may have been a Roman cistern, as the Roman road from Bremenium in Redesdale to the coast passes close by, whilst others believe it may have been a pagan holy place dedicated to mother earth. The pool was walled in and given its present shape in medieval times and was extensively restored in the late 18th century.

The name Holystone came into use early in the 12th century when a priory of Benedictine nuns was founded here by Robert Umfraville on the site of the present tiny 19th-century church of **St Mary**. Nothing remains of the priory except fragments of medieval masonry built into the walls of Mill Cottage, the churchyard wall and the outside wall of the chancel.

St Mungo's Well, sometimes known as Kentigern Well, stands just south of the church. There is no record of St Mungo ever having visited the area and the current well was built in the early 19th century. According to popular tradition it was the watering place for muggers (hawkers) who in late autumn took cartloads of Coquet salmon to local farms and villages.

Woodhouse Bastle stands in the grounds of Holystone Grange to the south of the village. It is one of the best and most complete bastles in the county and stands to full height. A stone inscribed with the date 1602 stands above the ground-floor doorway. The bastle has been restored by Northumberland National Park and can be reached from the road by a footpath.

Holystone Common, a forested outlier of the Cheviot Hills, is reached by quiet forest tracks south-west of the village, where there are a number of signed walks through the forest. Part of the area includes Holystone Burn Nature Reserve, an interesting valley filled with scrubland, juniper bushes and heather moorland. Here, too, is a group of tumuli known as **Five Barrows.** They were excavated in the 19th century and Bronze Age pottery, a cist and cremations were found, dating the site to between 1600 and 1000BC. There are many other prehistoric remains in the area, including a number of Iron Age hill forts and a line of stones known as **Five Kings.** These four standing stones are on a windswept moorland above Holystone Grange – the fifth has been used as a gatepost!

HORNCLIFFE [Berwick upon Tweed]

NU9249: 5 miles (8km) SW of Berwick

Perched on a red cliff above the River Tweed, where the river ceases to be tidal and navigable, is the village of Horncliffe. Charles I and Oliver Cromwell both camped at Horncliffe with their armies, as the ford was one of the lowest across the Tweed. Just to the south of the village is Horncliffe Dene, where a footpath follows steep-sided, wooded banks covered by ivy, honeysuckle and gorse to a waterfall and the remains of an old mill. There are some very attractive walks along the riverside from the village to the famous Union Chain Bridge.

The **Union Chain Bridge**, a mile (1.5km) downstream, was built in 1820 and the first suspension bridge to carry commercial traffic. It spans the River Tweed, a distance of 390ft (120m). On the English side the suspension chains are set into a massive abutment carved into the red sandstone cliff. They cross to a stone arch on the other side of the river, making a magnificent gateway into Scotland. It was designed by Sir Samuel Brown, a captain in the Royal Navy, who invented a new kind of link made of wrought iron. This enabled the link bars to be no more than 5cm (2 inches) in diameter and allowed larger suspension bridges to be built.

Chain Bridge Honey Farm has over 1000 colonies of bees kept in apiaries throughout the Scottish Borders and North Northumberland. Its visitor centre explores bees and aspects of bee-keeping. The farm sells a wide range of products including honey, beeswax candles and cosmetics.

HOWICK (Alnwick)

NU2517: 5½ miles (9km) NE of Alnwick

The small hamlet of Howick stands

close to one of the finest stretches of the Northumberland coast, possessing some of the most unusual geological formations in the country. The current hamlet consists of a long row of Tudor-style estate cottages. Just east of Howick is an 18th-century cottage that was remodelled for the Grey family as a bathing house. Rock steps lead from the cottage to a small, quarried bathing pool.

The church of **St Michael** stands in the grounds of Howick Hall by an attractive wooded ravine crossed by a bridge. It was built in 1749 but remodelled in the 19th century. In the church is a memorial to Charles, the second Earl Grey, of the Great Reform Act of 1832 fame. In the graveyard is a tall cross commemorating Albert Henry George, fourth Earl Grey (1851-1917), who was Governor General of Canada between 1904 and 1911 and involved in the early administration of Rhodesia (Zimbabwe).

Howick Hall is built on the site of a medieval pele tower which was pulled down in 1780 and replaced by the current elegant house, home of the Grey family. The gardens were partly designed by Wyatt and include an area of mixed woodland with a collection of monkey-puzzle trees, flowering shrubs and rhododendron borders. The gardens are open to the public between Easter and September.

HUMBLETON [Berwick upon Tweed]

NT9728: 1 mile (2km) NW of Wooler

This hamlet of modern cottages below Humbleton Hill sits on the site of a much larger village, the remains of which can be seen in the humps and bumps in the nearby fields. In medieval times there was a church, mill and village green. In the 19th century wealthy landowners bought out the freeholders, who moved away and the village declined. Women from the surrounding area came into the village and broke up the headstones in the churchyard because the sandstone is said to have made excellent scouring blocks for cleaning hearths, floors and doorsteps.

Above the hamlet is **Humbleton Hill,** which on the summit has the remains of a massive prehistoric hill fort. The settlement contained at least eleven houses, sheltered by an enclosure wall 13ft (4m) thick. Close by are the remains of terracing for crops and of burial cairns, signifying the hill was in continuous occupation over a long period of time.

North-east of the hamlet is the site of the **Battle of Hamildon Hill,** which was fought on Milfield Plain on September 13th 1402 between the English and Scottish armies. A large boulder a short distance from the A697, probably a prehistoric standing stone, marks the site. It was a bitter and bloody battle. The 10,000 Scots under Archibald Earl of Douglas were no match for the English archers; 800 Scots were killed and another 500 drowned trying to cross the Tweed. The battle ended in victory for the English and their leader Harry (Hotspur) Percy, who avenged his humiliating defeat by the Scots at the Battle of Otterburn in 1388.

HUMSHAUGH [Tynedale]

NY9271: 5 miles (8km) NW of Hexham

This small village stands on the slopes of the North Tyne valley, with pretty grey-stone cottages lining its main street. This leads to a pleasant open square at the top of the village. The village church of **St Peter** dates from 1818 and is a simple and attractive building.

Haughton Castle lies just north of the village on a bend in the River Tyne and dates from the 13th century. It is half hidden by trees, but its five turrets can be seen rising from the battlement walls. The castle is remarkable for its unusual long, thin shape. The castle suffered frequent sacking and burning during the Border troubles and was partially destroyed by Liddlesdale raiders in 1542 and subsequently abandoned. The castle was extensively restored in the 19th century by Dobson and Anthony Salvin, who added the west wing and the turrets.

Haughton Mill, just east of the castle, is now partly demolished, but was once a paper mill. Built in 1788, the mill was used to make paper for forged notes called assignats, a currency issued by the revolutionary government in France. The forgeries were part of an unsuccessful expedition into Flanders led by the Duke of York in 1793 with the aim of destabilising the French government.

ILDERTON [Berwick upon Tweed]

NU0121: 4½ miles (7km) SE of Wooler

Ilderton is an excellent example of a self-contained medieval farm town rebuilt in the 18th and 19th centuries, with a single farm and its associated massive buildings. The **church of St Michael,** built in pink sandstone, is late 18th century but incorporates the lower part of the 13th-century west tower of the previous church, which was burnt down by the Scots in 1300.

On the hills above Ilderton lie a number of interesting prehistoric remains including a stone circle at **Threestoneburn**. Thirteen stones are visible, but only five are still standing. Closer to the village, on Rosedon Edge, there are traces of prehistoric earthworks and two Iron Age urns were found here.

Lilburn Tower stands north of the village. It was designed by John Dobson in Tudor style in 1828-9 and was once the home of Admiral Collingwood. Close by is the original 15th-century Lilburn tower, now in ruins as is the Norman chapel which stands beside it. Here was found a gravestone 7½ft (2.3m) long and carrying the name Alexander, thought to be a Scottish noble who fell in battle.

INGOE [Castle Morpeth]

NZ0374: 7 miles (11km) NE of Corbridge

Ingoe is a small hamlet which has a standing stone and a number of hut circles nearby. Known as the Warrior Stone, it stands almost 6½ft tall and is decorated with cup marks. A number of Bronze Age finds were made near Ingoe in 1860.

INGRAM [Berwick upon Tweed]

NU0117: 8 miles (13km) S of Wooler

Ingram is a secluded hamlet which sits snugly alone on the south bank of the River Breamish, at the foot of Ewe Hill. As a natural gateway into the Cheviot Hills, Ingram was a frequent target for Scots and robber gangs who terrorised the district for hundreds of years. Ingram was provided with a tower of defence against these violent raids and in 1514 it held a garrison of forty men. The building stood close to the river and has now disappeared, its structure gradually undermined by flood water.

The tiny village is clustered around the **church of St Michael,** which is tucked among the trees above the stony bed of the river. The lower part of the church dates from Norman times but its overall appearance has changed dramatically over the last two hundred years. The whole structure was pulled down and re-erected in Victorian times when parts of the building became unsafe. The tower was shorn of its spire in 1803.

The bridge over the River Breamish is known as **Peggy Bell's Bridge** and was built in 1910. Previously the only way across the river was by a ford that was impassable after heavy rain. Flood water prevented the Adamson family getting to Doncaster for the St Leger and so they provided the money for a bridge. Peggy Bell was a shepherd's daughter from Greensidehill and used the bridge everyday to get to school. The school is now the National Park Information Centre and contains an excellent exhibition on the numerous hut circles, prehistoric forts and deserted medieval villages found on the nearby moors. Sites include Haystack Hill, Hartside and Knock Hill, and perhaps the most evocative sites in the valley – Borough Law, Greaves Ash and Wether Hill.

Borough Law, a promontory fort with two massive stone ramparts, is perched steeply to the left of the road above the Breamish Gorge. It was built about 2300 years ago, partly for defence reasons and partly for prestige. The faint traces of hut circles can still be seen within its enclosure, probably from the Roman period.

Wether Hill is perhaps the best example of an Iron Age hill fort in Northumberland. Its double ramparts enclose a settlement. Excavations have revealed the circular foundations of about twenty tightly packed timber houses. Close by are the distinctive ridge and furrow medieval field patterns.

Greaves Ash, near Linhope Farm and the impressive Linhope Spout waterfall at the head of the Breamish valley, is the largest prehistoric complex of its kind in Northumberland. It consists of forty huts occupied from Iron Age to Roman times. A medieval farmstead is superimposed upon the circle.

KIELDER [Tynedale]

NY6393: 14 miles (22km) NW of Bellingham

This Forestry Commission village near the head of the Tyne valley and close to Kielder Reservoir was built in 1950s to provide accommodation for forestry workers working in an area that was once expansive moorland. The first trees were planted in 1929 in the Upper

Kielder Water

Tyne valley, though the bulk of afforestation occurred between 1940 and 1970 and now covers around 72,520 hectares of reclaimed heath and moorland. These four forests – Kielder, Falstone, Wark and Redesdale – represent one of Europe's largest man-made forests. The key crops are Sitka spruce on wet peaty sites and Norwegian spruce in more sheltered areas. In the valleys Douglas fir, red cedar and larch have been planted, and more recently oak, willow, rowan and ash have been introduced along riverbanks. Increasingly, the forest is being managed to encourage and maintain wildlife habitats, as well as provide a major recreational resource. Walking routes, bike and equestrian trails, sculpture and orienteering courses have been developed for visitors.

Kielder Castle, built in 1775, was a shooting lodge for the Duke of Northumberland. It now houses the Kielder Visitor Centre and contains exhibitions about the forest and its wildlife and timber production. Close by is the start of the Forest Drive, a toll road which runs through twelve miles of conifer plantation to join the A68 near Bryness.

South of the village is Bakethin Reservoir, an auxiliary reservoir of **Kielder Water**. Kielder Reservoir is Europe's largest man-made lake with 250 million gallons (1138 million litres) a day storage capacity. It provides water to North East England. The reservoir itself is 9 miles (14.5km) long, covering 50,625 hectares (125,000 acres) of the Upper Tyne valley and required the felling of one and a half million trees during its construction. The earth dam opened in 1982 is three-quarters of a mile (1km) long and generates sufficient water pressure to drive two electrical generators. At the eastern end of the reservoir is an information centre, Tower Knowe, operated by Northumbria Water.

Until 1958 one of the most scenic railways lines, the **Border Counties Railway**, followed the North Tyne valley into central Scotland. It crossed below Kielder village by a 'skew' viaduct that still stands and forms an attractive walkway by Bakethin Reservoir. Opened in 1862, this seven-span bridge was crenellated at the insistence of the Duke of Northumberland to match nearby Kielder Castle.

Four miles (7km) south-west of the village on the Scottish border is **Bloodybush.** It is on a former drove road along Arkenshaw Burn, between England and Scotland, and marked by a stone pillar of 1830. The site is said to have got its name from a massacre of Northumbrians who were on their way home from a raid into Liddesdale. The pillar gives details of the distances and tolls levied on drovers, cattle and sheep following the construction of a more formal road by Sir John Swinburne of Capheaton. This was to move his coal from his mine, the site of which is now under the reservoir. It is still possible to follow the line of the road by foot, following forest tracks.

Sculpture, Kielder Forest

KIRKNEWTON [Berwick upon Tweed]

NT9130: 5 miles (8km) NW of Wooler

Close to the confluence of the River Glen with Bowmount Water and the College Burn, Kirknewton is dominated by the remote empty landscapes of the Cheviot Hills. A compact border village of cottages with thick stone walls, it stands at the foot of Yeavering Bell, a northern outlier of the Cheviot Hills.

The Norman church of **St Gregory the Great** contains a remarkable stone carving thought to be Saxon, although it is probably Norman. It depicts the Adoration of the Virgin, in which the three Magi are shown to be wearing kilts. The church is Early English in style, although the tower and nave were altered in the late 1800s. The church has a unique tunnel-vaulted chancel and south transept built on walls barely 3ft high. **Josephine Bulter** (1828-1906), the Northumbrian social reformer, is buried in the churchyard. She was a crusader against the 'white slave trade' and the hypocrisy in the way women who had became prostitutes were treated. She worked to rehabilitate girls who for one reason or another had been forced into prostitution and successfully campaigned to change the law.

Kirknewton Station was built when the London North Eastern railway opened a branch line from Alnwick to Coldstream in 1887. Most of the line's income came from carrying agricultural livestock, potatoes and grain, so although it was closed to passenger service from 1930, the Wooler to Coldstream section continued for goods traffic until 1965.

The name of nearby **Yeavering Bell** is derived from the Anglo-Saxon name 'Gefrin' meaning 'hill of the goats'. There are still wild goats on the hillside. On the top of the hill is one of the largest Iron Age hill forts in Northumberland, extending over 5 hectares (12 acres) and providing magnificent views across the Milfield Plain to Scotland. Within the massive stone rubble walls of the hill fort, which run right round the summit, are hollows and level areas for 130 circular wooden houses. There is evidence on the south-facing slopes of the hillside of cultivated terraces, demonstrating that the area once enjoyed a much warmer climate. At the foot of Yeavering Bell is a prehistoric 10ft high standing stone known locally as the **Battle Stone.** It is said to commemorate a victory over the Scots in 1415.

Below the hill fort is thought to be the site of King Edwin's Palace of **Ad Gefrin**. He lived here in the 7th century and was the first Christian king of Northumbria. The palace was mentioned by Bede and evidence of buildings dating from this period and earlier has been found in excavations. A monument beside the road marks the site.

Coupland Palace, lying across the River Glen, is a tower with later additions dating from 1594. It is now a private residence, but its grounds are open to the public on advertised days.

KIRKWHELPINGTON [Tynedale]

NY9984: 13 miles (20km) W of Morpeth

Almost by-passed by the A696, Kirkwhelpington sits snugly on a mound overlooking the River Wansbeck. The village church of **St Bartholomew** stands on an island site surrounded by an attractive cluster of stone cottages. The church was founded in Norman times and for a short while John Hodgson, the Northumbria historian, was vicar here between 1823 and 1832. The squat perpendicular tower completes a simple, aisleless 13th-century nave and long chancel. Inside, despite Victorian restorations, the church maintains its medieval character with an impressive tower arch decorated with zigzag moulding and a simple stone font. Above the stone-tiled porch is an unusual worn sundial of 1764.

Inside the church is a memorial to **Sir Charles Parsons,** inventor of the steam turbine who lived nearby and was buried in the churchyard in 1931. The steam turbine was to revolutionise steam power production and was used in warships in the First World War as well as for passenger liners and cargo ships. Parsons was also a master of optics and at his works in Newcastle made telescopes for the observatories at Greenwich, Edinburgh, Toronto and Pretoria.

The **Kirkhale estate** is one mile (2km) south-east of the village. Its hall is Victorian and the tiny estate chapel dedicated to St Wilfrid is 14th century on Norman foundations. It was here that **Lancelot 'Capability' Brown** was born in 1715 and began his career as a landscape gardener in service to Sir William Loraine of Kirkhale. He was to become one of the greatest landscape gardeners of his age and was to become head gardener at Windsor for George III. Capability Brown designed the grounds of many of England's finest country houses.

LAMBLEY [Tynedale]

NY6858: 4 miles (7km) SE of Haltwhistle

A former colliery village set in the wooded South Tyne valley and overlooking a splendid thirteen-arch viaduct, one of the most magnificent railway structures in Northumberland. **Lambley viaduct** stands 35 metres (110ft) above the South Tyne river. When it was completed in 1852 it was the final link in the Alston to Haltwhistle railway, a branch of the Newcastle to Carlisle railway. The railway was built to aid the transport of lead from the ore fields around Alston and was originally intended to go as far as Nenthead and Weardale. By the mid-19th century the lead industry in the North Pennines had started its slow decline, but the railway continued providing a vital link for the remote communities of the South Tyne valley. The line eventually closed in 1976, causing an enormous uproar. The Lambley viaduct has recently been restored by the British Rail Property Board and is now owned by the North Pennines Heritage Trust. The line itself now forms the 10-mile (16km) South Tyne Trail between Alston and Featherstone, just south of Haltwhistle. At Alston, on the Cumbrian side of the border, the last two miles (3km) of the former line are used by the South Tynedale Railway, a narrow gauge steam railway which operates in the summer months.

The attractive little 19th-century church of **St Mary and St Patrick** has a chancel with fine stone vaulting and an elaborate wooden roof in the nave. In a tiny turret between the nave and chancel hangs a bell that is said to have come from the ruined nunnery washed away by the river in 1769. This Benedictine convent was founded in Norman times, but was burnt down in 1296 by the Scots under William Wallace.

LANGLEY [Tynedale]

2 miles (4km) SW of Haydon Bridge

Langley is a former lead-mining and colliery town, though little remains of its two 18th-century smelt mills which once dominated the village. The course of its remarkable horizontal flue can still be traced zigzagging its way south-east up the hillside to its terminal chimney on Stublick Moor and the large reservoir which supplied power to drive the furnace bellows is also evident. The old packhorse routes can still be followed south to the former lead mines. In the village the timber station of the now closed Allendale Branch railway (1867) is the village post office.

South of the village, screened by trees, are the battlements of **Langley Castle**. Its four square towers were magnificently restored in 1890 by Cadwallader John Bates, a local antiquarian. Now a hotel and restaurant, the castle was built in the angle of land between Dean Raw and Nagley Burns in 1350 by Sir Thomas de Lucy to protect himself and his property against the Scots. The castle was partly destroyed in 1405 by King Henry IV, in the course of putting down Archbishop Scrope's rebellion. It later passed to the Earls of Derwentwater, who were to forfeit it in 1716 following their support of the Jacobite rebellion.

On the A686, on the approach to Langley Castle, is a massive grey Celtic cross erected in 1883. The cross is in memory of two Jacobite Earls of Derwentwater, James and Charles, Viscounts of Langley, who were beheaded on Tower Hill, London on February 24th 1716 and December 8th 1746, for 'loyalty to their lawful sovereign'.

LESBURY [Alnwick]

NU2311: 3 miles (5km) SE of Alnwick

A straggling village built above the River Aln, which is crossed by a picturesque, old bridge which marks the point at which the Aln is still tidal. Its name is said to derive from 'Laece Burg', 'the town of the leech or physician', the reason for which is unknown. Like similar villages in the area, Lesbury was decimated by the Great Plague in the 17th century. Local inhabitants who had the disease were taken to a nearby moor and left to die under crude wicker shelters.

At the centre of the village is the fine Norman church of St Mary, which was restored by Salvin in 1846. Its square 13th-century tower is topped by a Victorian pyramidical roof and inside there is a fine 13th-century chancel with a roof of 15th-century oak beams decorated with carved bosses incorporating the Percy emblem.

LONGFRAMLINGTON [Alnwick]

NU1301: 9 miles (14km) SW of Alnwick

This village on the A697 has a fine Norman church and a picturesque row of cottages from the late 18th and early 19th centuries set alongside a pant. **St Mary's** dates from 1190 and is transitional in style, with an elegant Norman chancel arch decorated with waterleaf capitals and three detached pillars on either side of the nave. In the vestry is a delightful carved Jacobean chest with ten little trees carved in its cornice.

The route of the **Devil's Causeway**, a Roman road which ran between Hadrian's Wall and Tweedmouth on the Scottish Border, can easily be traced crossing farm land west of the village. At Brinkburn, when the River Coquet is low, the foundations appear of the Roman bridge which once carried the Devil's Causeway across the river.

Brinkburn Priory, lying in a sheltered meadow 2 miles south-west of the village, in a loop of the River Coquet, was founded in 1135 by the Lords of Mitford for a colony of Augustinian canons. It suffered greatly from Scottish raids and on one occasion the monks were so eager to celebrate their deliverance from the Scots that they rang the bells too soon, bringing their subsequent downfall and the dispatch of the bells into a nearby pool! After the Dissolution of the Monasteries in 1536, the Priory Church was still used by local people until the 18th century, when it fell into disrepair. The church was beautifully restored in 1857. Its peaceful, serene setting has attracted painters such as J.W. Turner. Brinkburn Priory is now in the care of English Heritage and is a particularly good example of early Gothic architecture, with lofty, pointed arches contrasting with a three finely carved late Norman doorways decorated with chevron, zigzags and beakheads in the nave.

LONGHORSLEY [Castle Morpeth]

NZ1494: 6 miles (10km) NW of Morpeth

The village sits astride the A697 on a ridge overlooking the Coquet valley. At its centre is an immaculate village green lined with white posts and chains. At the western end is a well-preserved pele tower, **Horsely Tower**. Now a private residence, it dates from the 16th century and has a vaulted basement and spiral staircase leading to the battlements, from where there are views to Druridge Bay, the Simonside Hills and the Cheviots.

The old village church stood some distance south of the village and is now in ruins. Its porch has been re-erected on the current church of St Helen, which was formerly the Victorian village school.

LONGHOUGHTON (Alnwick)

NU2415: 4 miles (6km) NE of Alnwick

Longhoughton is a small agricultural and quarrying village built alongside the East Coast mainline, but its railway station closed long ago. The church of **St Peter and Paul** has a Norman tower with 5ft thick walls guarded by four gargoyles in the shape of wolves' heads just below the battlements, which were added in the 19th century. The tower was used as a refuge during the Border Wars. The rest of the church is mostly Victorian, using building material from the original church, though the Norman arch survives. South of the chancel arch is a large squint.

West of the village is an impressive inland cliff of basalt known as **Ratcheugh Crag**, crowned with a mock ruin. The area is famous for its wild flowers and from here there are magnificent views down the coast to Coquet Island and west towards the Cheviots.

LOWICK [Berwick upon Tweed]

NU0139: 8½ miles (14km) S of Berwick upon Tweed

Built on an east-west axis along the old Roman road to Tweedmouth, Lowick, like its name, feels Scottish. Lowick was once the centre of an extensive lime trade, and an old limekiln still stands north of the village at Old Dryburn. A long, thin village, Lowick contains a Roman Catholic church (1861) and large Presbyterian chapel (1821), as well as St John's (1794), the Anglican church.

East of Lowick are the **Kyloe Hills**, an area of rugged crags covered by forestry plantation from where there are superb views of Holy Island, the Farnes, Bamburgh and Dunstanburgh. Standing on a cliff edge are the remains of an ancient hill fort estimated to be around 2000 years old. Below, in West Kyloe, is the church of St Nicholas (1792), which contains a late, undecorated Saxon cross in the churchyard. Half a mile away is East Kyloe Tower, a medieval pele tower which belonged to the Greys. Attached to the current farm buildings, the tower was inhabited until 1633. Now in ruins, it has lost its upper storey but still retains its vaulted basement and 8ft thick walls.

LOW-NEWTON-BY-THE SEA [Alnwick]

NU2424: 3 miles (5km) NE of Beadnell

The village of Low Newton consists of an open-ended square of cream-washed cottages set around a green and looking out to sea across the beach of Newton Haven. This small 18th-century fishing village, complete with a shop and the Ship Inn, is now owned by the National Trust. There are walks to Newton Pool Bird Reserve and along the sands to Embleton Point and Dunstanburgh Castle.

LUCKER [Berwick upon Tweed]

NU1530: 3 miles (5km) SW of Bamburgh

The name of this hamlet is said to be Norse and means 'marsh frequented by sandpipers'. That marsh was drained in the mid-19th century. It was during that process that a remarkable discovery was made when a small oak box fastened by copper nails was unearthed. In it were twenty-two Roman copper coins, some horse harnesses and a brass apothecary's scale and beam. The coins indicate that the finds date from the 3rd century AD.

LYNEMOUTH [Castle Morpeth]

NZ2991: 2½ miles (4km) NW of Newbiggin-by-the- Sea

This small industrial town stands on the south banks of the River Lyne. Lynemouth was developed in the 1920s and 30s and linked to the former Lynemouth colliery and a massive aluminium smelting plant. The Miners' Institute stands at the centre of the town. On the sandy coastline, fossilised tree stumps sometimes appear after winter gales. Further west there are attractive walks through a wooded dene along the banks of the River Lyne.

MATFEN [Castle Morpeth]

NZ0271: 5½ miles (9km) NE of Corbridge

A bubbling stream runs through the centre of this attractive estate village with its sycamore-lined green. Most of the cottages are 19th century, as is the church of **Holy Trinity** which stands on a slight rise above the green, crowned with an elegant spire. **Matfen Hall**, Elizabethan in style, was built between 1823 and 32 for Sir Edward Blackett, a member of a prominent Northumbrian family. It is now a Cheshire home. The current village stands west of the old village, which in 1623 was abandoned after a severe visitation of the plague caused the survivors to burn their homes and build a new village.

The **Stob Stone** stands a mile south of the village, on the roadside opposite a farm. It stands 7ft high and is rather weather-worn, but the cup and rings markings which decorate it can still be seen.

MELDON [Castle Morpeth]

NZ1183: 5 miles (8km) W of Morpeth

This tiny rural hamlet stands in lush farmland above the River Wansbeck with views to the Simonside and Cheviot Hills. Meldon's tiny village church of **St John** originates from the 13th century and was restored by Dobson in the 19th century. The nave and chancel are one, with small lancet windows and pointed bellcote. Inside the church is an effigy to Sir William Fenwick, dressed in full armour, who died during the Commonwealth.

Meldon Park, a square-fronted villa, lies one mile away from the village on the other side of the River Wansbeck. It was built by John Dobson in 1832. The grounds are particularly fine and include a large walled garden and a woodland walk with colourful rhododendrons. The grounds are open to the public on advertised days during the summer months.

MICKLEY SQUARE [Tynedale]

NZ0762: 1½ miles (2km) SW of Prudhoe

Mickley Square consists of a few 19th-century buildings and 1930s semis strung along the A695. To the north of the village, in an attractive setting above the River Tyne, is **Cherryburn**, the birthplace of the famous Northumbrian engraver and naturalist, Thomas Bewick. Born in 1753, Bewick was a self-taught draughtsman who became an apprentice to Ralph Beilby, the Newcastle engravers, and was later to have a shop in the precincts of St Nicholas's Church.

The tiny, sparse Bewick family cottage has been restored and is now in the care of the National Trust. A small museum has been created in the nearby 19th-century farmhouse (a later home of the Bewick family). It explores his famous works and life and includes extracts from the *General History of Quadrupeds* (1790), *History of British Birds* (1797) and *Fables of Aesop* (1784). In the printing house visitors can watch demonstrations of hand printing from wooden blocks, and in the adjacent farmyard there are various animals including a pig, donkey and chickens.

On the main road is the small **Bewick Studios Printmaking Museum,** which gives free demonstrations in a reconstructed 19th-century printmaking workshop.

MITFORD [Castle Morpeth]

NZ1786: 2 miles (3km) W of Morpeth

An unspoilt village west of Morpeth, Mitford sits above two wooded valleys at the confluence of the River Wansbeck with the River Font. Two stately bridges lead in and out of the village. The southern one, Foss Bridge, leads to **Mitford Castle**, whose ruined five-sided keep was destroyed by the Scots around 1318, but still dominates the skyline on a rocky ridge above the river. The castle was built about 1118 by William Betram, the founder of Brinkburn Priory, and was occupied in 1175 by William the Lyon, and by King John in 1216. It was later destroyed by the Scots under Alexander III in 1318. In the 19th century the castle was made into a romantic ruin that could be viewed from Mitford Hall.

The Norman church **St Mary Magdalene** stands separate from the main village of Mitford, which moved to its present location after the original village was sacked and burned by King John in 1216. King John laid waste to the North, burning castles and towns during his squabble with the barons. Most of the church was reconstructed in 1875 but several 11th- and 12th-century features remain, including a fine example of a priest's door on the outside wall of the chancel with typical Norman chevron moulding.

Mitford Hall, like Meldon Park a few miles further west, is an example of a Dobson country house in neoclassical style. It was built in 1828 and almost encircled by the River Wansbeck. It was built for Betram Osbaldeston Mitford and replaced the old, largely 16th-century manor house which stands just south-west of the church and is now mainly in ruins.

MORPETH [Castle Morpeth]

NZ1985: 15 miles (24 km) N of Newcastle

This attractive old market town set either side of the River Wansbeck is now the county town. In the summer rowing boats can be seen gentle cruising along in Carlisle Park, with its tree-lined paths, ducks and children's play area contrasting with its busy main street. Bridge Street, Oldgate and Newgate are lined with Georgian buildings, including the fine town hall built in 1714 to the design of John Vanbrugh, though subsequently altered after a fire in1869. In Oldgate stands the Clock Tower, one of the very few examples in England of an isolated belfry. It dates back to the early 17th century although older masonry was used. It still tolls the curfew at 8 o'clock each evening. Here, too, is Collingwood House, the home of **Admiral Lord Collingwood** who commanded the fleet at the Battle of Trafalgar after Nelson's death.

Morpeth developed as a crossing point on the river. It was later to become an important stopping place on the Great North Road and there are still many fine coaching inns in the town. The main bridge was built as a toll bridge in 1831 by Telford (to the design of Dobson). It was part of a big improvement scheme for the main road between London and Edinburgh. The narrow medieval bridge that ran alongside was blown up in 1834 to force people to use the new toll bridge. The present cast-iron footbridge, which in

Old Chantry at Morpeth

summer is attractively bedecked with flowers, was built on the stone piers of this bridge and opened in 1869.

In medieval times, bridge tolls were collected in the 13th-century Chantry Buildings. These now house the Tourist Information Centre, a Northumbrian crafts centre and the acclaimed **Bagpipe Museum.** The chantry was founded by Richard of Morpeth in 1296 as a chapel for private prayer, at the same time as the medieval bridge. The building was altered in 1738. There was a grammar school in the chantry from the early 14th century until 1858. The museum explores the history and development of Northumbrian small pipes. The exhibition looks at similar instruments from other parts of the globe, and there is plenty of opportunity to listen to different types of music of this surprisingly versatile instrument.

On the opposite side of the river is the site of Morpeth Castle. The first castle seems to have been on Ha' Hill in Carlisle Park, south of the river, and founded by William de Merlay after the Norman Conquest. This was sacked by King John in 1216 during his squabble with the barons, and the subsequent castle built on Castle Hill suffered further at the hands of the Scottish raiders and in the English Civil War, when it was taken for the king. The only surviving remains are the 15th-century gatehouse and motte and bailey. Opposite Castle Square is the massive courthouse designed by John Dobson of Newcastle in grand Gothic style. This was the gatehouse to the county jail (1829-81) and has in more recent times been used as a restaurant.

St Mary's Parish Church, also south of the river, is mostly 14th century built on Norman foundations. There are some fine features dating from this period, including some beautifully carved sedilia (seats for priests) in the chancel and an east window that still contains some original glass. The watchtower next to the churchyard was built in 1837 to guard against body snatchers. A local custom still practised is that the church gates are tied at weddings until the bridegroom pays a toll.

In the churchyard is buried the famous suffragette **Emily Wilding Davison**, who on the day of 1913 Derby threw herself at the feet of the King's horse Anmer and died of her injuries. Davison was born at Longhorsley in 1872, and after graduating at London University joined Emmeline Pankhurst's Social and Political Union.

Nearly a mile west of the town centre, along an attractive riverside path are the ruins of **Newminster Abbey**, a Cistercian foundation established around 1137 by Ranulph de Merlay. It was ravaged by the Scots soon after its completion but following its reconstruction it was to became exceedingly powerful up to the Dissolution of the Monasteries. Little can now be seen of the abbey except some lengths of low wall and grass-covered mounds.

NETHERWITTON [Castle Morpeth]

NZ1090: 7 miles (11km) NW of Morpeth

This hamlet is built around an attractive old bridge crossing the River Font, where it meets Ewesley Burn. The present manor house, **Netherwitton Hall,** dates from the late 17th century. There has been a dwelling here since the 14th century, when its first tenant was Roger Thornton, a prosperous Newcastle merchant. His descendants were paid £95 5s.6d compensation by Oliver Cromwell for allowing him and his horsemen to camp overnight in the grounds in 1651. The party consisted of his horse guards, nine regiments of foot, two of dragoons and all their baggage.

The church of **St Giles** retains its 15th-century chancel, but was much altered in the 18th and 19th centuries. The remains of a Georgian mill stand on the riverbank close to the bridge. It began as a cotton mill and was then converted to woollens and later a sawmill, before becoming housing in the late 1980s. Two miles (3km) north-west of Netherwitton, on an attractive wooded side lane, is **Nunnykirk Hall**, considered to be one of John Dobson's finest works.

NEWBIGGIN-BY-THE-SEA [Wansbeck]

NZ3087: 4½ miles (7km) N of Blyth

Newbiggin's cliff-top church spire, standing in a treeless headland north of the town, provides a prominent local landmark for shipping. In danger from falling into the sea through constant cliff erosion, **St Bartholomew's** dates from the 13th and 14th centuries. During the Second World War its roof was damaged and its windows blown out by mines exploding on the rocks. It is said that the Lindisfarne monks founded the church, but various features in the church suggest that it may have had earlier origins. The church contains a collection of over twenty medieval grave slabs dating from the 13th century, of which the most interesting is one marked by shears and keys, denoting that it was the grave of a woman.

Once a colliery town and grain port, Newbiggin is now an attractive seaside town set along a sandy bay with some holiday and camping amenities.

NEWBROUGH [Tynedale]

NY8767: 4½ miles (7km) NW of Hexham

An attractive former colliery community set in wooded surroundings, Newbrough contains a number of fine Victorian buildings including its rather surprising Italianate town hall. The 19th-century parish church of **St Peter** is on the site of a Roman fort that was built to guard the Roman road, Stanegate, and stood midway between Corbridge and Vindolana. The only ancient relic in the church is a medieval grave slab carved with a sword.

The neighbouring village of **Fourstones** stands on the line of Stanegate and overlooks the South Tyne. It may derive its name from the four Roman altars that once stood there. Just two miles (3km) north of the village is Carrawburgh, the site of the Roman fort **Brocolitia** on Hadrian's Wall. Little is now visible of the fort, but close by are the remains of the temple to Mithras where three altars were found, and where replicas now stand. Mithraism was an Eastern religion which had a following among some

Roman soldiers. It was a religion that focused on the struggle between light and darkness. A full reconstruction of this temple is displayed in the Museum of Antiquities, Newcastle upon Tyne.

NEWTON [Tynedale]

NZ0264: 3 miles (5km) NE of Corbridge

A pleasant hamlet of stone houses with the Victorian church of St James sheltered by the woodlands of Mowden Hall School, formerly Newton Hall and built in the 19th century. In its grounds, Newton Hall Tower survived until 1980, when it was demolished by a local man who wanted the stone. Newton Hall Tower was part of a medieval mansion of the Lile family.

NEWTON ON THE MOOR [Alnwick]

NU1605: 5 miles (8km) S of Alnwick

Built on the crest of land between the Aln and Coquet rivers, the village of Newton on the Moor consists of mostly single-storey 18th-century cottages, once the homes of coal miners and quarry men. The local inn, unusually named Cook and Barker, takes its name from the original proprietors. **Newton Hall,** south of the village, was built in 1772 and altered in the 19th century. The hall is a private residence but the magnificent gardens, which include a fine walled garden, are open to the public twice a year under the Northumbria Gardens scheme. Close to Newton Hall are the **Waterloo Stones**, three stone slabs, the central one commemorating the Battle of Waterloo, flanked by memorials to two French seamen said to have drowned off the Northumberland coast.

NINEBANKS [Tynedale]

NY7853: 4 miles (6km) SW of Allendale Town

This pretty hamlet in the West Allen valley is thought to derive its name from the line of the land around it. Originally a Saxon property, the parish of Ninebanks was part of the dowry of Ethelreda, wife of Egfrith, King of Northumbria, but was given to the church in AD674. Today, Ninebanks consists of a few stone cottages and the church of St Mark (1871), which stands just south of the village. Next to the village post office is Ninebanks Tower, which dates from the 16th century. The remains of a carved stone shield on a second-floor window links the tower with Sir Thomas Dacre of Hexhamshire.

NORHAM [Berwick upon Tweed]

NT9047: 7 miles (11km) SW of Berwick upon Tweed

This historic border village was until 1836 the capital of Norhamshire, part of the County Palatine of Durham. Lying amidst rich meadowland in a loop on the south bank of the River Tweed, Norham looks across to Scotland. In medieval times Norham was the setting of many of the Border War conflicts and its castle was the inspiration behind Sir Walter Scott's *Marmion*.

In the centre of the village is a triangular green with stone cottages surrounding it, some of which are attractively whitewashed and have red-tiled roofs. In the centre of the green is a pinnacled market cross (1870) on a medieval base of six steps. A weather vane in the shape of a fish celebrates local salmon fishing. Each year the Blessing of the Nets Ceremony heralds the start of the fishing season in February. Traditionally, the vicar is always is offered the first fish caught.

The ruins of **Norham Castle** stand at the east end of the main street, on high ground overlooking the rocky bank of the River Tweed below. Its massive rose-coloured walls and great Norman keep standing nearly 30 metres (90ft) high make an impressive sight against a curtain of beech trees. Now in the care of English Heritage, the castle was built by Bishop Flambard as part of the northern defences of the Palatine of Durham in the early 12th century. After destruction by the Scots, Norham was rebuilt by Bishop Hugh de Puiset in the late 12th century. He was responsible for the walls and keep. The castle had to withstand many Scottish onslaughts throughout the 13th and 14th centuries and was once thought to be impregnable until it was finally stormed by troops under James IV of Scotland in 1513, just prior to the Battle of Flodden. The castle was later returned to the English and partially repaired. After an attack in 1530 the castle was abandoned, and fell into decay when Elizabeth I decided it was no longer required. The core of the Norman masonry still survives, as do the ruins of the gatehouse and turrets, and the remains of the buttery, pantry and kitchen, with its huge oven added in Tudor times.

Up a lane leading from the north corner of the village green is **St Cuthbert's Church**. It was founded in 830 by Eafrith, Bishop of Lindisfarne who built a wooden church to hold the remains of St Ceolwulf, the converted Christian king to whom the Venerable Bede dedicated his *Ecclesiastical History of England*. The Norman bishop Ranulph Flambard built the first stone church on this site, which suffered constant attack from the Scots. The present building dates mainly from the 19th century but a number of Norman parts have survived, notably the chancel and south arcade. The south arcade consists of five bays with moulded arches divided by mighty piers, each crowed with an elaborately carved capital. The chancel with an elegant Norman arch still has its five original windows, and on the south side these are decorated with zigzags and beakhead ornamentation. The richly carved vicar's stall, organ screen and pulpit with fruit, cherubs and Gothic motifs are made from dark oak and date from the 17th century. They were brought here from Durham Cathedral in the 19th century.

Norham Station Museum is based in the original signal box, booking office and porter's room of the former station on the Tweedmouth to Kelso line, a branch line of the York, Newcastle and Berwick railway opened in 1851. The museum contains a model railway and an interesting collection of Victoriana.

OGLE [Castle Morpeth]

NZ1378: 4 miles (7km) NW of Ponteland

A tiny hamlet of grey-stone cottages, Ogle was once a much larger village.

The earthworks of former medieval dwellings and ridge-and-furrow field systems can still be seen north of the current settlement. Ogle Castle, which is now a much restored, primarily 16th-century building, dates back to the 14th century when it belonged to the Ogle family. In 1346, after the Battle of Neville's Cross, John de Coupland brought David Bruce, King of Scotland as a prisoner to the castle.

OLD BEWICK [Berwick upon Tweed]

NU0621: 9 miles (15km) NW of Alnwick

The name of this hamlet, Old Bewick, probably derives from the Old English 'bes-wic', meaning 'bee farm'. The hamlet lies under the bracken-covered hill beneath an ancient fort. The hill fort dates from the second century BC and consists of two horseshoe-shaped defences lying side by side with three visible sets of stone walls and ditches rising to the central arena where the huts once stood. Close by are some excellent examples of cup and ring-marked stones, perhaps symbolising the importance of this site from which there are superb views over the Vale of Whittingham.

Just north of the village, alongside Kirkburn, is one of the most attractive small churches in Northumberland. **Holy Trinity,** hidden among trees, is said to have been founded by Queen Matilda, wife of Henry I, in memory of her father, Malcolm King of the Scots, who had been killed nearby at Alnwick. The church was later in possession of the powerful Tynemouth Priory, which owned much of the land in the North. The oldest surviving part of the church is 12th century and retains much of its Norman character, despite being damaged by the Scots in the 14th century and in later storms, leading it to be restored twice, once in 1695 and then in the middle of the 19th century. The beautiful Norman chancel and apse arches have been colourfully restored with a motif of stars on a blue background with bands of red and gold lettering. The carved chancel arch is particularly fine. Its north capital is carved with two grinning beasts' faces intertwined with a twisted tree. Against the north wall of the chancel is a canopied 14th-century worn figure of a woman dressed in mantle and kirtle with her head on a cushion. In the porch there are the fragments of an Anglo-Saxon cross and several medieval tombstones.

OTTERBURN [Alnwick]

NY8893: 7 miles (11km) NE of Bellingham

Below the wide sweep of hills of Redesdale, on the busy A68 to Scotland, Otterburn stands defiant amidst a bleak and empty landscape. It is the setting of the famous Battle of Otterburn fought in August 1388. It marked the climax of a bitter quarrel between the Percy family of England and Douglas family of Scotland and was fought at night by moonlight. The battle became the stuff of legend and was commemorated by the English ballad *Chevy Chase* and by the Scottish ballad *The Battle of Otterburn*. During the battle the young Earl of Douglas was killed and Harry Percy, Hotspur in Shakespeare's *Henry IV*, was taken prisoner, causing the rout of the English forces.

The supposed site of the battle, just south of Otterburn Hall (now a hotel), is marked by Percy's Cross, which stands in a grove of fir trees. The cross was erected here in 1777, but the base of the cross is medieval. From Otterburn there are a number of stone markers known as Golden Posts, which indicate ancient routes across the Borders and are probably Roman in origin. Local tradition insists that these were erected at places where the Earl of Douglas's body rested during its journey back to Melrose Abbey.

Otterburn Mill, just south of the village, stands alongside the River Rede. There has been a mill on this site for at least 700 years, and the present building dates from the mid-18th century. Otterburn Mill became renowned for its tweeds and blankets using local wool, particularly during the middle of the 20th century. On site production stopped in 1976 but the mill still contains much of its original machinery, including the restored 19th-century water turbine and original tenterhooks used for drying and stretching woven cloth. There is an exhibition area, coffee shop and retail area selling the famous Otterburn pram rug.

The **Padon Monument** lies four miles (6km) west of Otterburn along an unclassified moorland road just off the Pennine Way and stands on Padon Moor. The beehive-shaped stone tower was built by followers of the Scottish Covenantor Alexander Padon, who held religious meetings on the spot to escape persecution. It is claimed that each member of the congregation carried a stone to every service until the tower was finished.

OVINGHAM [Tynedale]

NZ0863: 1 mile (2km) NW of Prudhoe

This quiet village has stood on the north banks of the Tyne since Anglo-Saxon times. It is joined to its neighbour Prudhoe by a narrow iron bridge across the River Tyne. A packhorse way once came through the village, crossing Whittle Burn, a tributary of the Tyne, and a 17th-century packhorse bridge still spans the stream, whose waters were once famed for bleaching linen.

The weather-worn vicarage is early 17th century and stands on the site of a cell of Hexham Priory. The flood marks of 1771 and 1851 can still be seen on the walls of the garden terraces. Ovingham has a particularly fine church, **St Mary's**, founded by the Augustinian canons. The tower is partly Saxon and has been constructed using Roman stone. The interior is mostly 13th century and includes a fine 13th-century font with a large round bowl, fragments of a 10th-century stone cross and a number of early gravestones carved with crosses, swords and shears. George Stephenson's mother, Mabel Stephenson, is buried in the churchyard, as is Thomas Bewick (1753-1828), the famous Northumbrian ornithologist and engraver. Bewick is commemorated with a plain stone slab in the porch where as a boy he used to cover the walls with chalk drawings.

Ovingham holds an annual goose fair

on the third Saturday in June and other traditional Northumbrian events.

PONTELAND [Castle Morpeth]

NZ1672: 7½ miles (12km) NW of Newcastle upon Tyne

Ponteland has become a popular commuting suburb of Newcastle within easy reach of the airport. At its centre, divided by the River Pont from which the village derives its name, stand two fine buildings – the Blackburn Inn and St Mary's Church. The inn is a converted 17th-century manor house belonging to the Errington family, which itself was built from a medieval pele tower. This was the setting for the signing of a peace treaty between the English and the Scots in 1244. An underground tunnel is said to have once linked the Blackburn Inn with the church of St Mary, which stands opposite. It is still possible to drink in the vaulted basement of the old tower.

St Mary's dates from Norman times and the lower part of the tower dates from that period but is built of Roman stone. The upper section is 14th century. The western doorway has a round Norman arch with two rows of zigzag moulding whilst the chancel arch is decorated with two intriguing corbels, one with two scowling faces and the other with the heads of a man and a woman separated by a writhing serpent. They represent Adam and Eve before and after the fall.

On the main road, in the garden of the vicarage stands a three-storey vicar's pele in a grove of trees which is said to be 14th century, though the existing remains are 16th century.

Kirkley Hall, 2½ miles (4km) west of Ponteland was once the home of the Ogle family and is now an agricultural college set within 4 hectares (10 acres) of grounds. The grounds are open to the public and include ornamental gardens with over 35,000 different species of labelled plants, trees and shrubs, including the national collection of beech, ivy and willow, as well as greenhouses and a wildlife pond.

POWBURN [Alnwick]

NU0616: 8 miles (13km) WNW of Alnwick

The hamlet of Powburn derives its name form a Scottish word meaning 'slow-moving stream' and refers to a tributary of the River Breamish which flows through the village. The Roman road, the Devil's Causeway, passed close to the hamlet, guarded by a Roman fort. The stone of this fort was probably used to construct 14th-century **Crawley Tower**, one of the oldest pele towers in the county and now converted into a farmhouse. Crawley Tower may have been built on pre-Roman earthworks and commands a strategic position above the Breamish valley.

PRUDHOE [Tynedale]

NZ0963: 6 miles (10km) E of Corbridge

A workaday town on a wooded hillside overlooking the south bank of the Tyne, Prudhoe grew up around its castle. **Prudhoe Castle** commanded the principle north-south route through Northumberland, and is built on a natural strong defensive site above a river cliff of the Tyne. Its Norman keep, with

10ft (3m) thick walls were well able to withstand an assault by King William of Scotland, who attacked the castle in 1173 and 1174. The castle was built in late Norman times by Ordinel de Umfraville, but passed to the Percy family, the Dukes of Northumberland, in the 14th century. Now in the care of English Heritage, the castle is entered through a splendid 12th-century gatehouse, the oldest surviving part of the castle. The gatehouse contains a converted 13th-century chapel with an oriel window above the altar, thought to be one of the oldest examples in England. In the 19th century a manor house was built within the castle and now contains an exhibition on Northumberland castles.

Prudhoe Castle

REDESMOUTH [Tynedale]

NY8682: 2 miles (3km) SE of Bellingham

A hamlet above the confluence of the River Rede with the North Tyne river, Redesmouth stands on the old western terminus of the Wansbeck Railway (1862) which ran from Morpeth. Here it formed a junction with the Border Counties line, which survived until the 1950s for passengers and closed to freight in 1963.

RIDING MILL [Tynedale]

NZ0161: 3 miles (5km) SE of Corbridge

A small residential town on the south banks of the River Tyne, Riding Mill has been a popular commuting village for Newcastle since Victorian times when its station opened. The site of the original mill that gave the town its name dates back to the 14th century. The current building was used for corn milling until 1900, when it became a sawmill. It is now a private house. The Manor House dates from the 17th century, as does the Wellington Inn, which has the date 1660 carved above the original doorway. The Duke of Wellington Inn is said to have once been a famous meeting place for witches from all over the country. Four of them were tried in 1673, and the usual evidence was presented of dancing with the Devil, the transformation of cats and aerial riding – not on broomsticks but on eggs and dishes. All the accused were acquitted.

Close to the town is a huge pumping station which pumps water from the Tyne under pressure. This is used to augment Kielder Reservoir stocks, 27 miles (43km) north-west of here and 700ft (213m) above the level of the Tyne.

RIDSDALE [Tynedale]

NY9084: 4½ miles (7km) NE of Bellingham

The tiny hamlet of Ridsdale on the A68 overlooks Redesdale. It is dominated by a castle-like structure on the west of the road, easily mistaken for a Borders stronghold. It is, in fact, a ruined engine house that powered the Ridsdale Ironworks. These ironworks supplied the iron used in the construction of the High Level Bridge in Newcastle. Ridsdale Ironworks was built in 1836 and closed in 1848. The site was later acquired by W.G. Armstrong, who dismantled it around 1865. In its heyday the ironworks comprised of three furnaces, the engine house and an adjoining boiler house. Nearby were coke ovens and calcining kilns, with reservoirs across the road. A network of tramways linked the site with nearby sources of ironstone, limestone and coke.

ROCHESTER [Tynedale]

NY8398: 4½ miles (8km) NW of Otterburn

The village of Rochester is strung out along the main A68. The village is dominated by the Redesdale Army Camp, which forms part of the **Otterburn Training Area**, a series of artillery ranges and practice areas covering 70 square miles (18,130 ha) of wild moorland between Windy Gayle

Ridsdale ironworks in snow

on the Scottish border and Otterburn in the south. There is limited public access to the area, but guides are available showing recommended routes and rights of way. The Otterburn Training Area was established in 1911 when the War Office bought 7600 hectares (19,000 acres) of land in Redesdale as an artillery range for the newly formed Territorial Army. Horse-drawn artillery batteries came from all over Britain by train to West Woodburn and marched up Dere Street, now the A68, to camp in huts and tents. The artillery ranges were extended in the Second World War and the Otterburn Training Area is now the largest live-firing range in Britain. It is estimated that 30,000 British and NATO soldiers come here each year to train for periods of between two days and two weeks.

The Brigantium Centre in Rochester is a new visitor attraction exploring the archaeology of Northumberland. It displays reconstructions of stone circles, Celtic heads and Iron Age huts and links to the Roman remains at High Rochester nearby (see High Rochester for details).

ROCK [Alnwick]

NU2020: 5 miles (8km) N of Alnwick

A small agricultural village of estate cottages set back from a pleasant green. The compact **church of St Philip and St James** dates from the Norman period and the west doorway and chancel are both decorated in typical zigzag moulding. The church was considerably altered in the 19th century, when the apse was designed by Anthony Salvin whilst he was working at Alnwick Castle. In the chancel there are monuments to the Swinhoe family, Lords of Rock; Charles Bosanquet (d.1850), Governor of the Canada Land Company and Colonel John Salkeld who served Charles I. King Charles and his army stayed at Rock on the march north towards Scotland in the First Bishop's War.

Rock Hall is now a youth hostel built on the remains of a pele tower, but subsequently much altered. In 1549 it was the headquarters of a band of Spanish mercenaries under Sir Julian Romero and used in the various Border skirmishes. Later the hall became the home of the Proctors, agricultural pioneers who in the 18th century developed a system for using turnips in winter for cattle fodder.

ROTHBURY [Alnwick]

NU0501: 11 miles (18km) SW of Alnwick

Rothbury, on the north banks of the River Coquet, is an ancient market town and gateway to Northumberland National Park. The main street is lined with traditional grey-stone houses that in the 18th century would have been thatched with heather cut from the surrounding moorland. At its centre is an attractive sloping green shaded by mature sycamores planted in the late 19th century, when the town established itself as a popular Victorian health resort.

Rothbury can trace its origins back to the 12th century, when it was first mentioned in documents as Routhabiria ('Routha's town'). In the surrounding hills there is evidence of much earlier occupation, with the remains of Iron

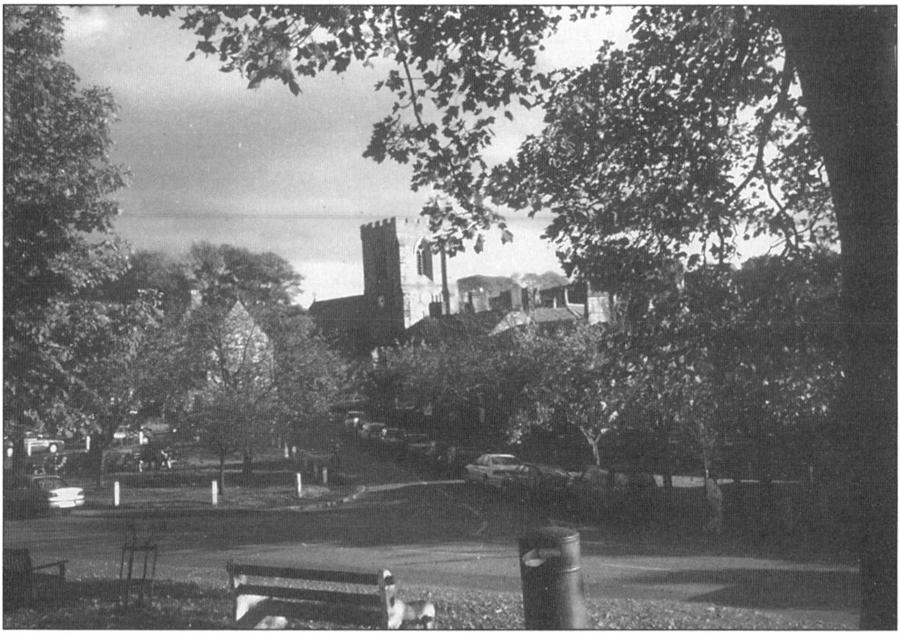

Rothbury

Age and Bronze Age settlements, hill forts, cairns and cup and ring markings. King John granted Rothbury a market charter in 1291 and for many years this was held in a stone shelter on the village green. The shelter was demolished in 1827. It was here the town declared its support for the Jacobite cause when a proclamation was read for James III in 1715. The present cross, dedicated to Lord Armstrong, was erected in 1902 and fashioned in the Arts and Crafts style of the period.

Rothbury's original monastic church was destroyed either by the Vikings or Normans, however, the eastern part of the building seems to have survived to become the foundation of a new church in the 13th century, part of which can be seen in the chancel. In the 18th century **All Saints** had galleries, dormer windows and a three-decked pulpit, but these were all dismantled in the restoration of 1850. The church contains a magnificent font. The bowl, dating from 1664, stands on a beautifully carved red sandstone Saxon cross shaft dating from the beginning of the 9th century (the head is in the Museum of Antiquities in Newcastle). The two broad faces of the shaft are carved with the Ascension scene and with a design of Saxon meshed-knot weave. On the narrow faces is a depiction of the fall of Man and on the reverse images of Hell, with withering serpents devouring animals and trapping a naked human figure. The cemetery to the left of the church is built on the site of Rothbury Castle, demolished in 1869. Lord Armstrong of Cragside is buried here.

Below the church is a medieval bridge with three arches spanning the River Coquet. It has been much altered by subsequent widening and the modern bridge deck rests on the arches of a

17th-century packhorse bridge extended in the 18th century to cope with a widening river. The passing of the Corn Laws caused a massive increase in traffic over the bridge when it became part of the important corn road (toll road) from Hexham and the Tyne valley to the port of Alnmouth.

To the east, the River Coquet flows through a narrow, wooded gorge called the **Thrum,** an attractive ¾-mile (1km) walk from the town. The gap was once much narrower, attracting local youths to leap across the gap and leading to several fatalities. The channel was widened to discourage further attempts. Standing close by is old Thrum Mill – no longer working but in good order. It dates from the 18th century.

Overlooking the Thrum is **Cragside,** the great Victorian house built in the style of a Rhineland Castle. Cragside was designed by Norman Shaw for the Newcastle industrialist, the first Lord Armstrong and stands in the middle of a 567-hectare (1400-acre) estate planted with rhododendrons and trees and accessed by over forty miles of drives and footpaths. The National Trust now owns Cragside and among the thirty rooms on show are the wonderful Turkish-style baths and grand drawing room with a massive chimney piece carved in Italian marble. The house was one of the first to be lit by electricity, which was water-powered and included hydraulic lifts and a hydraulic spit in the kitchen. Armstrong developed his own hydroelectricity system in the grounds with man-made lakes and miles of underground piping which can be explored in the 1½-mile (2km) 'Power Circuit' walk that includes the restored hydraulic machinery.

Cragside

South of Rothbury are the **Simonside Hills,** an area of red sandstone crags and heather-clad slopes dominated by the conifer plantation of Harwood Forest. This was once part of a medieval deer park, Newtown Park, which was enclosed by Robert Rogerson in 1275. Occasionally roe deer can be still be seen, but little now remains of the wall that once surrounded the extensive reserve except for a section between Lordenshaw and Tosson.

The summit of **Lordenshaw** is crowned by a hill fort built 2500 years ago and providing extensive views across the Upper Coquet valley. The fort defences consist of three concentric rings of banks and ditches, originally topped with a wooden palisade around a small living area of no more than 200ft (61m) across. The remains of houses built inside the walls of the fort can also be seen. Nearby are a series of ancient cup and ring rock carvings, including the Horseshoe Rock. These date from the New Stone Age (Neolithic) and are probably around 5000 years old. The surrounding area also contains number of Bronze Age burial mounds.

RYAL [Castle Morpeth]

NZ0174: 6½ miles (10km) NNE of Corbridge

A tiny hamlet of stone-roofed houses, Ryal has a interesting church, **All Saints,** built on the site of a 12th-century chapel of ease. The current church, erected in 1870, has reused some of the medieval masonry, including the Norman chancel arch with its fine scalloped capitals and saltire crosses. Set into the west wall are nineteen medieval gravestones carved with floral crosses and swords. The pulpit is a memorial to the people who died at the beginning of the 20th century during the construction of the Whittington tunnel and aqueduct works designed to carry water to Newcastle.

South-west of the village is a green hill called **Grindstone Law**, on whose summit sit the remains of a prehistoric fort with a mound and ditch clearly visible.

SCREMERSTON [Berwick upon Tweed]

NU0049: 2½ miles (4km) S of Berwick upon Tweed

A quiet former mining village which is now a suburb of Berwick upon Tweed. Just south of the village is the massive beam pumping engine house of Scremerston old mine. Erected in 1840, it is surmounted by a cast-iron panelled water tank. Another former industry was lime making, and the remains of limekilns can be seen by the sea at the foot of a cliff at Seahouse.

At Far Skeer, south-west of the village, is a coastal Nature Reserve reached by minor road. Saltpan Rocks, near the reserve, is where salt was once made by evaporating sea water.

SEAHOUSES [Berwick upon Tweed]

NU2232: 12 miles (19km) NE of Alnwick

Fish and chip shops selling freshly caught cod and haddock seem to dominate this small holiday and fishing village. Seahouses did not exist until 1889 when the harbour was built to boost the local fishing industry and the older village of North Sunderland, further inland, became a quiet backwater. The harbour still houses the local fishing fleet and from here there are boat trips to the Farne Islands.

In the centre of the village is the relatively new **Marine Life and Fishing Heritage Centre** which explores what life is like in the fishing industry, both at sea and ashore. The exhibition includes displays of crab and lobster fishing, large fish tanks of herring and a reconstruction of a smokehouse. Just north of the village are **Aidan's Dunes,** 24 hectares (60 acres) of flower-covered sand dunes now in the care of the National Trust.

The **Farne Islands** are a group of

over thirty basaltic islands and rocks formed from the final outlier of Great Whin Sill. The islands divide into two main groups – Inner and Outer Farnes – and their actual number varies according to the state of tide. The largest island, Farne, gives its name to a group of beautiful treeless islands renowned for their flora and wildlife. Over seventeen species of birds, including puffins, kittiwakes, guillemots, fulmares, terns and eider duck, are found on the islands, which are important summer breeding grounds. Eider ducks are known in Northumberland as St Cuthbert's chicks. A large colony of grey seals also use the islands as a breeding ground.

The first inhabitant on the islands was St Aidan, the Bishop of Lindisfarne (AD635-651), who built a simple stone cell on Farne Island to pray and meditate in peace. His successor St Cuthbert also made the island his home between 676 and 685. In 1246 a small Benedictine cell from Durham was established on this site and the remains can still be seen, including **St Cuthbert's Church.** This small chapel built in 1370 was restored in 1845.The oak panelling, stalls and screens in the current chapel came from Durham Cathedral during the restoration. Across the courtyard is a second church, St Mary's, of which only its base course remains. It is now used as a National Trust Information Centre, but was probably contemporary with St Cuthbert's and may have been a pilgrimage chapel.

A pele tower was constructed on the island around 1500 by Thomas Castell, Prior of Durham, and a fire lit on its roof to warn ships. It was used after the Dissolution as part of the coastal defences. There was also a beacon on Brownsman Island, which was later the site of the first lighthouse, constructed in 1809. The present lighthouse stands on Longstone Island. It is painted in red and white and was built in 1826. It was the home of the Darling family at the time of the famous rescue of the SS *Forfarshire* in 1838.

For centuries the Farnes have been an easy source of eggs for collectors, which caused an alarming decline in the bird population by the late 19th century. The Farne Islands Association was formed in 1880 to protect the wildlife of the islands. In 1925 the National Trust acquired the Farnes with Longshore lighthouse, and in 1964 the islands became a bird sanctuary. It is possible to visit two of the islands – Staple and Inner Farne – though access is limited in the breeding season. Information about sailings and tickets can be obtained from the National Trust Information Centre and shop in Seahouses.

SEATON SLUICE [Blyth Valley]

NZ3376: 4½ miles (7km) E of Cramlington

Seaton Sluice was once a thriving coal port and industrial centre, but is now a rather attractive sleepy village with a green set along a deep cut from which the village derives its current name. Originally it was known as Hartley Pans, after a salt pan fired with local coal situated at the mouth of Seaton Burn and dating back to the 13th century. It adopted its new name when a sluice was built to flush out silting in the harbour in the 17th century.

The improvements to the harbour began in 1660 when Sir Ralph Delaval built a pier and wharves with the intention of establishing Seaton Sluice as a port for shipping locally produced salt. To overcome the silting of the narrow Seaton Burn channel, huge sluice gates were built just upstream of the current road bridge. At high tide the sluices were opened to let the force of water scour the channel. In the 1860s the harbour proved too small for the number of ships using it so Thomas Delaval cut a new entrance, with a wharf along the north side and lock gates at either end. It was used to export coal and glass bottles that were produced locally. The harbour was last used commercially in 1871. The cut has been restored in recent years and is 275 metres (900ft) long, 9 metres (30ft) wide and 16 metres (52ft) deep from the cliff top.

St Mary's Lighthouse, which stands on an island south of the village, is just over the North Tyneside border. Built in 1897-8, there has been a lighthouse here since medieval times. The lighthouse is no longer in use but owned by the local authority who maintain a small exhibition and shop. St Mary's can be accessed at low tide via a causeway running from the mainland.

A footpath along Seaton Burn links the village to **Holywell Dene,** part of the ancient woodland that once covered this part of what is now Tyneside. In spring the woodland is carpeted with wild flowers including bluebells and wood anemones. Overlooking the Dene are the ruins of a folly called **Starlight Castle,** which is said to have been built in 24 hours by Sir Francis Delaval as a 100-guinea wager in the 1750s.

A mile inland is **Seaton Deleval Hall**, built in the Palladian style by Sir John Vanbrugh between 1718 and 1729 and considered to be one of his finest buildings. It was designed for Admiral George Deleval. High Tuscan columns support a high portico that forms the central block. Either side is an ornate wing, one of which is a stable block. The hall was damaged by fire in 1725 and 1822. Following the last fire the hall fell into disrepair, but its current owner, Lord Hastings, a descendant of the Delevals, has spent considerable time and effort on its restoration. The hall and gardens are open to the public at advertised times. In the grounds of the hall is the Norman **Chapel of Our Lady,** said to have been built by Hubert Delaval who went on the first crusade. The chapel has an air of simple beauty, with plain white walls. Two superb Norman arches have survived in the chancel and sanctuary, standing one behind the other and carved with zigzag moulding. Originally a family chapel, Our Lady is now used as the parish church for Seaton Delaval, an ex-colliery town.

SHILBOTTLE [Alnwick]

NU1908: 3 miles (5km) S of Alnwick

A long, straggling village grouped around a village green which, despite its three pants, is more akin to a series of fields. Shilbottle contains a number of 18th-century cottages, but a lot of development dates from the 20th century. The church of **St James** is sheltered by a belt of trees and has a central battlement tower. The original 12th-century church was rebuilt in 1875. The current building reuses the Norman south doorway with its billet moulding and the former chancel arch in the organ chamber. The roof, ceilings and walls are attractively panelled and the pulpit and stalls are richly carved with fruit and foliage. The former vicarage, consists of a house adjoined to a former medieval pele tower. South-west of the village is Beacon Hill, which as the name suggests was used in the Napoleonic Wars to signal potential danger with a bonfire.

SIMONBURN [Tynedale]

NY8773: 7½ miles (12km) NW of Hexham

A North Tyne estate village of white-washed stone houses clustered around a large, tree-shaded green, Simonburn was created when the old village on the banks of the river was swept away in 1740 to make room for **Nunwick Hall**. The hall was built to the design of Daniel Garrett, and subsequently altered by Bonomi. It contains fine rococo decoration. It is a private residence but the gardens are famous for their alpines and herbaceous borders and these are open to the public on advertised days.

The church of **St Mungo,** built of grey stone, dates from the 13th century but was substantially rebuilt in the 18th and 19th centuries. It has an unusual floor which slopes towards the altar and a fine chancel which was restored by Anthony Salvin between 1863 and 1864. Reset in the south wall of the sanctuary is a massive 13th-century double piscina, which would have been used by the priest to wash his hands before Communion. In the north aisle is a carved marble relief in memory of Robert and Elizabeth Allgood. It is by Matthew Noble, best known for the Albert Memorial in the centre of Manchester. In the porch there is part of a Saxon cross shaft that is beautifully carved with vine scrolls.

Simonburn Castle lies just west of village in the middle of woods. The ruins of the 14th-century tower house can be reached by public footpath from opposite Burn House. The tower was partly rebuilt in the18th century as a folly for the neighbouring Nunwick Hall, but the 10ft thick defensive walls can still be traced on the north-west side.

North-west of the village, the road to Wark Forest passes close to Ravensheugh crags and the enigmatic **Goatstones**, a stone circle with four stones, one of which bears cup and ring markings dating from 1600-1000 BC.

STAMFORDHAM [Castle Morpeth]

NZ0772: 5½ miles (9km) E of Ponteland

A pretty 18th-century village with two rows of houses built either side of a long sloping green, Stamfordham is now a conservation area. The name of this village literally means 'stony ford ham' and refers to the days before a bridge was built, when the only crossing of the Pont was by a stony ford. A weekly cattle market was held on the green from the early 18th century and a butter cross still stands in the middle of the green. It was erected in 1735 by Sir

John Swinburne of Capheaton. Close by is the village lock-up, which was used to the beginning of the 20th century. At the far end of the green is the 13th-century church of **St Mary**, an impressive building with a massive tower. The chancel has long, elegant lancet windows and a pointed arch dating from about 1220. In the chancel lie the effigy of a robed priest dating from the 13th century (probably the earliest in the county) and the legless figure of Sir John Felton, a survivor of the Battle of Otterburn Field in 1338 who lived to be High Sheriff of Northumberland. Across the river from the present village are the remains of the older settlement of Stamfordham – now a series of earthworks.

STANNINGTON [Castle Morpeth]

NZ2179: 4 miles (7km) S of Morpeth

Now by-passed by the Great North Road (A1), Stannington is a handsome village and quiet backwater popular with Newcastle commuters. The tall west tower of its church, **St Mary the Virgin,** dominates the village. The church was rebuilt in 1871, replacing a medieval one. A few relics of the former church remain including a Norman font, an interesting collection of medieval cross slabs and, outside the south wall, a massive stone coffin. From the village there are fine walks along Stannington Vale along the banks of the River Blyth to Plessey Woods.

Blagdon Hall stands south of the village and is the seat of the Ridley family, one of the most notable Northumberland families. The current house dates from the 18th century and stands in gardens that were remodelled by Sir Edwin Lutyens in 1938. The gardens are occasionally open to the public as part of the Northumberland Gardens scheme.

STONEHAUGH [Tynedale]

NY7976: 4½ miles (7km) W of Wark

A purpose-built early 1950s Forest Commission village in Wark Forest, Stonehaugh is accessed by a remote side road across Broadpool Common. The Pennine Way crosses through the village near Ladyhill, where forestry workers have erected a series of whimsical totem poles. North of the village the Pennine Way passes **Comyn's Cross,** which was erected by a Scottish family who owned land nearby in the 13th and 14th centuries. One of the members, John Comyn – Red of Badenoch, was murdered by the followers of Robert the Bruce when they met at Dumfries in 1306 to settle who was to be Scottish king.

In the village there is a car park and camping facilities and a number of waymarked forest walks including the Warksburn Forest Trail. There are some attractive walks along **Warksburn Gorge** to Holywell Cottage, named after a nearby sulphur well reputed to cure 'ague, gravel and other obstructions'. A group of derelict buildings at **Roses Bower** near Warksburn gorge were once the home of the Milburns, one of the main North Tyne families renowned for Reiving activities. The buildings include the remains of a 17th-century bastle and an outside netty toilet, known as the 'Long

Drop'. This was an earth closet suspended 12 metres (40ft) above the gorge with only a basic toilet seat between the user and rocks below!

Haining Deer Farm is set deep in Wark Forest and is open to visitors during the summer months.

THIRWALL [Tynedale]

NY6566: 4 miles (6km) NW of Haltwhistle

The hamlet of Thirwall grew around the castle whose dramatic ruins stand high above the steep west bank of Tipalt Burn. The castle probably dates from the early 14th century when troubles with the Scots began in earnest. It is built entirely from stone taken from the Roman wall, the line of which runs below the castle. Overlooking one of the main routes of the Scots, the castle was designed to withstand attack. Its walls are about 3 metres (9ft) thick and there are very few windows.

THOCKRINGTON [Tynedale]

NY9579: 6 miles (10km) NE of Chollerford

This isolated hamlet consists of little more than a farm tucked away among trees and the church of **St Aidan** standing on an outcrop of Whin Sill. Thockrington is surrounded by the traces of a larger village that is said to have been deserted as a result of an outbreak of typhoid in the early 19th century.

The very remoteness of the church with its splendid views over to the ridge of Hadrian's Wall gives it a special atmosphere. Externally the church has a rather top-heavy bellcote supported by the neck of a stepped buttress against its west wall and this probably dates from Stuart or Hanoverian times. Inside the church has kept its beautifully simple Norman interior. A splendid obelisk monument, which is visible for miles around, stands in the graveyard and here, too, is the grave of **Lord Beveridge** (d.1963).

The countryside around Thockrington contains several lakes and reservoirs and the scars of old quarrying. To the north is Sweethope Lough, an attractive lake close to the source of the River Wansbeck. Colt Crag Reservoir, fringed with conifers, provides water for Newcastle.

THROPTON [Alnwick]

NU0202: 2 miles (3km) W of Rothbury

The village stands in Upper Coquetdale and is divided by Wreigh Burn, a tributary of the Coquet crossed by a hogbacked bridge. Neat stone houses line both sides of the street and at its west end is Thropton Tower, a 15th-century pele tower which is now converted into a modern residence. Nearby is the Three Wheat Heads Inn, an attractive 18th-century coaching inn. All Saints, a Catholic church, dates from the late 18th and early 19th centuries and has an unusual three-arch screen which separates the chancel from the nave. At the east end of the village, Physic Lane climbs past attractive flower-bedecked cottages and a drinking well to become a green track leading to unenclosed heather moorland. There are lovely walks from Wreighburn Bridge to the Coquet following riverside paths.

ULGHAM [Castle Morpeth]

NZ2392: 1½ miles (2km) SW of Widdrington

Beside the village street are the remains of a medieval stone cross where markets are said to have been held during the plague in Morpeth. Ulgham's church, St John the Baptist, is set on a steep bank above the River Lyne. A predominantly neo-Norman church built in Victorian times, in the north aisle is a crude Norman stone relief of a knight on horseback, apparently protecting a lady from two birds shown above her shoulder.

WALL [Tynedale]

NY9168: 3 miles (5km) NW of Hexham

The village of Wall is grouped around a large square green on which some of the houses and the church of **St George** (1895) form an island. Several of the older houses appear to be bastle houses, and it is thought that Wall in the 16th and 17th centuries was a defensive village with an enclosed green into which animals could be driven at night. The village gives its name to the local inn on the main Hexham to Chollerford road (A6079), which forms a back lane to the village.

Planetrees stands just north of the village and is the modern name of a stretch of Hadrian's Wall where the reduction from the originally planned broad wall (10 Roman feet or 2.9 metres wide) to the narrow wall (6 Roman feet, 1.7 metres) can clearly be seen, with the narrow wall sitting on the broader foundations. This section of the Wall leads down Brunton Bank towards **Brunton Turret**. This is one of the best-preserved turrets on Hadrian's Wall, standing over 2 metres high (6½ft).

The reputed site of the Battle of **Heavensfield,** where King Oswald (later canonised) of Northumbria defeated the North Welsh King Caedwalla and West Britons in 634, lies north-east of the village, marked by a wooden roadside cross on the B6318. A swift Christian evangelising of the North followed Oswald's victory. Close to the cross is the isolated chapel of **St Oswald,** standing on a small hill screened by trees. Built in 1737, the chapel commemorates the battle. Inside is a Roman altar carved with vine branches and grapes, which is thought to have been used as a socket for the previous wooden cross erected outside the chapel. In the porch are a number of ancient gravestones and carvings, including the head of Christ.

WARDEN [Tynedale]

NZ9166: 2 miles (3km) NW of Hexham

Warden is a secluded hamlet on the wooded slopes of High Warden Hill, a sandstone summit 587ft (179m) above sea level. The hill is crowned by an extensive Iron Age hill fort which commanded the North and South Tyne valleys. Its name is appropriately derived from 'weard-dun' or 'watch hill'.

The village church of **St Michael and All Angels** stands in an oval churchyard. The church dates from Saxon times and has been traditionally associated with the site of an oratory of St John of Beverley (in the diocese of York) founded in the 8th century. The west tower is Saxon, with typical irregular quoins and three primitive narrow window openings. It appears that stones from Hadrian's Wall have been used in the tower arch and nave, possibly from the Roman fort at Chesters. In the porch is a remarkable carved grave slab which is thought to have come from a Roman altar; it contains a full length figure with outstretched arms and could be a depiction of Victory. The church was altered in 1765, when the belfry was added. The chancel was medievalised in Victorian style in 1889. Outside stands a 7th-century parish cross that may have been a boundary sanctuary cross associated with Hexham Priory. The charming Boat Side Inn stands close to the bridge over the South Tyne. Just to the west is one of the oldest paper mills in the country, dating from 1763.

WARK ON TYNE [Tynedale]

NY8677: 9½ miles (15km) NW of Hexham

Wark was once the capital of Tynedale and dates back to Saxon times when it is said that the Christian King of Northumbria, Elfwald, was murdered here in 788. Set alongside one of the prettiest sections of the North Tyne valley, a steep grassy bank is all that remains of the once massive Norman motte and bailey fortifications which were built as part of the North of England defences against the Scots. The castle became the base for the head of the lordship of Wark but between 1150 and 1295, when Tynedale was part of Scotland, the Scottish kings held court here.

The rest of village spreads around the crossroads with the B6320, with the road on the eastern side leading to a pleasant village green surrounded by neat grey-stone houses. One of these buildings is a 16th-century farmhouse. The **church of St Michael** was built in 1818 by the Commissioners of Greenwich Hospital, who after the break up of the Derwentwater Estate after the 1715 rebellion owned the huge parish of Simonburn to which Wark belonged. Similar churches were also built at Greysteads, Humshaugh and Thorneyburn. In the churchyard is a memorial to Abel Chapman, the naturalist.

One and a half miles (2km) south of Wark is **Chipchase Castle,** a 14th-century tower house incorporated within a Jacobean building which is now a private residence. This was the residence of the Keeper of Tynedale, responsible not only for protecting the local population against Scottish raids but also for maintaining law and order.

WARK ON TWEED [Berwick upon Tweed]

NT8238: 2 miles (3km) SW of Coldstream

This tranquil village on the south bank of the Tweed and the setting of one of the great Border fortresses was described in 1541 as a 'jewwl of noysance (nuisance)' against the Scots. Little now remains of the 12th-century motte and bailey castle which once commanded a ford across the River Tweed. Throughout much of the Border Wars **Wark Castle** was under the control of the English crown. It had to withstand frequent attacks and was besieged by the Scots eleven times between 1136 and 1523. It was built in the early 12th century by Walter d'Espec at the eastern end of a long ridge of gravel called the Kaim, a natural glacial ridge that runs nearly a mile towards Carham. Shortly before the Battle of Flodden the castle was partly destroyed by James IV. It was rebuilt between 1517 and 1519, creating a huge four-storey keep, and was used as an artillery fort during the 16th century. Today, the visible remains of the castle consist of the motte, surmounted by the massive stonework ring of the artillery platform, and the fragments of the south-west tower and enclosing curtain wall.

According to popular legend, in 1346 Wark Castle was being defended by the beautiful Countess of Salisbury and Edward III turned north to her aid. After successfully driving off the Scots the King was entertained at a victory ball given by the Countess. During the ball she lost her garter. The King, nobly retrieving it, fastened it on his own leg and uttered the now famous words, 'Honi soit qui mal y pense.' (Evil to him who evil thinks.) These words were subsequently to become the motto of the order of the garter.

East of the village is the site of the bloody **Battle of Carham** fought in 1018. Malcolm II of Scotland and Owain the Bald of Strathclyde defeated an English army under Uhtred, Earl of Northumberland.

WARKWORTH [Alnwick]

NU2406: 6 miles (10km) SE of Alnwick

The ancient fortified town of Warkworth is built on a rocky spur within a tight loop of the Coquet close to the river mouth. The main street descends from the castle to the river and is lined with mellow stone buildings. Alongside the river is the beautiful Norman church of St Laurence with its 14th-century spire. Crossing the river are two bridges, a modern concrete structure and a two-arched medieval stone bridge with a guardhouse at its southern end, making it one of England's few fortified bridges. It is now open only to pedestrians.

The first record of a church on this site was in 738AD when Ceolwulf, the King of Northumbria, gave the church with the rest of the village of Wercewode, as it was then known, to the monastery at Lindisfarne. The **church of St Laurence** has a 90-ft Norman nave, the longest in Northumberland. The nave, built with strong, thick walls, would have been used as a refuge during times of trou-

Warkworth's medieval bridge

ble, as in 1174. Duncan, Earl of Fife, accompanying the Scottish King William the Lyon entered Warkworth and put to death three hundred of its inhabitants who had taken refuge within the church. The nave is flanked by a southern aisle that was added in the 15th century by the Percys. At the west end of the aisle is the effigy of a knight, known only as Sir Hugh, with his feet on a lion. His identity is uncertain but he was probably linked with the castle. The chancel is entered through a Norman horseshoe-shaped arch and has an exceptionally fine vaulted ceiling, its ribs marked by zigzag decoration. In a recess in the southern wall is part of a Saxon gravestone with a cross. The iron altar railings are 17th century.

Warkworth Castle dates from the 12th century and is thought to have been established by Henry, son of David I of Scotland, after he had been created Earl of Northumberland in 1138. The castle later passed to the FitzRodger family and in 1332 the Percys. The Percys used the castle as their main residence until the late 17th century, and it was here that Hotspur, Earl of Northumberland, was brought up. Later the Percys were responsible for Victorian restorations made under Anthony Salvin, reroofing part of the keep and adding framed windows. It is now in the care of English Heritage.

In Shakespeare's *Henry IV,* Warkworth is referred to as 'a worm-eated hold of rugged stone', but even in its partially ruined state it is one of the most imposing fortifications in the country. The castle is dominated by its magnificent 14th-century keep which towers above the skyline. From the great keep there are views over the mouth of the Coquet to the lighthouse on Coquet Island. Inside, the guardroom and stores are on the ground floor and above are the kitchens with their huge fireplaces, the great hall, stone gallery and the chapel. A third storey above housed a number of chambers. The keep is surrounded by a curtain wall entered through the Great Gate Tower and within its walls are various buildings, including a dungeon, great hall and the Lion Tower crowned with the heraldic emblem of the Percys.

A half-mile (1km) beautiful riverside pathway follows the steep-sided valley beneath the castle and leads to a hermit's cell carved from the sandstone cliff. **The Hermitage** is accessed by a small ferry boat operated by English Heritage on certain days of the week during the summer. Dating from the 14th century, legend has it that young Betram de Bothal accidentally slew his brother and his intended bride and in penance gave away all his worldly goods and confined himself to the banks of the River Coquet to pray for salvation. An inscription just inside the entrance reads, "fuerunt mihi lacrymae panes nocte et die." (Tears have been my portion day and night.) In use until the 16th century, The Hermitage consists of a tiny chapel with a vaulted ceiling and scenes from the Passion carved into the rock. It is reached by a flight of steps and a dark sacristy with a plain vault lies behind the chapel. Between the two is a cusped squint so designed that the chaplain could see the altar from his bed at the west end of the sacristy. Adjacent to the chapel are the remains of domestic buildings which included a kitchen and solar and date from the 15th century

WEST WOODBURN [Tynedale]

NY8986: 4 miles (6km) NE of Bellingham

West Woodburn is linked to its neighbour East Woodburn by a quiet lane which follows the south bank of the River Rede. Close to the village is the site of the Roman fort of **Habitancum** (Risingham), which was built on a bend of the Roman road Dere Street where it crossed the River Rede. It was one of the first outposts north-west of Hadrian's Wall and was a day's march from Corstopitum (Corbridge). The only remains are a series of grassy mounds standing in private land. Dating from the 2nd century, the fort was probably only continuously occupied from the 3rd century to the early 4th century, when it housed 1000 cavalry and a unit of mounted scouts. A Roman milestone has been re-erected north of the village and marks the boundary of Northumberland National Park.

South of the village, close to Parkhead Farm, are the remains of a Roman sculpture known as **Robin of Risingham**. It is thought to be either a representation of Emperor Commodus in the role of Hercules or a local Celtic god Cocidius, who was adopted by the Roman garrison. The sculpture was smashed by the local landowner in 1819 because trespassing sightseers infuriated him. The upper part was used for gateposts and two plump legs are all that remain today. A smaller representation of the complete Robin stands close to the original remains, erected in 1983 by the Redesdale Society.

At East Woodburn there are two bastle houses. One of which has a fragment of the Roman altar from Risingham built into its fabric. It contains an inscription to the native god Cocidius and a hunting scene.

WHALTON [Castle Morpeth]

NZ1381: 5 miles (8km) SW of Morpeth

Whalton's broad main street, a conservation area, consists of a series of spacious green verges dotted with trees and lined with neat rows of brown-stone cottages. The village was originally built around a pele tower, which was incorporated into the former rectory. In the main street stands the long, grey-roofed Manor House, which was originally three cottages until it was converted for their owner by Sir Edwin Lutyens in 1908. The buildings are linked by a picturesque archway that gives a wonderful glimpse of the gardens designed by Gertrude Jekyll.

St Mary Magdalene is built of light-coloured stone and is remarkably wide for its length. The church is of Norman origin, but the building is mostly 13th century. Between the chancel and the Ogle Chapel is an interesting pillar made up of four widely spaced filleted shafts topped with carved human faces and linked by huge dog-tooth mouldings. The church was restored in 1908.

Whalton is one of the few places in Northumberland to light a bale fire.

'Bale' derives from a Saxon word meaning 'great fire' and is a pagan tradition going back to Saxon and Viking times. The lighting of the fire on July 4th is accompanied by demonstrations of folk dancing, the playing of Northumbrian pipes, and sword dancing.

WHITFIELD [Tynedale]

NY7758: 10 miles (16km) SW of Hexham

A secluded village above the wooded valley of West Allen, Whitfield stands on the Plenmeller road. It is built around a small village green and the church of St John (1790). Whitfield's other church, Holy Trinity with its tall spire, stands on the main A686 route to Alston in the valley bottom. This church dates from 1860 and was partly built from stone of the older church of St John. Next to Holy Trinity are estate offices, a pub, village shop and blacksmith's shop collectively known as Bearsbridge. They belong to the Whitfield estate. Whitfield Hall dates from the mid-18th century and is built on the site of a medieval fortified tower. It is now part of an 8000-hectare (20,000 acre) estate.

A toll-house can still be seen south of Whitfield Hall and dates from the days when the road was the old Hexham to Alston turnpike road (1778). North of the village the turnpike crossed the steep gorge of the River Allen, a short distance downstream from where the East and West Allen rivers join by Cupola bridge. This three-arch stone bridge is said to take its name from the lead-smelting mill which stood nearby.

WHITTINGHAM [Alnwick]

NU0611: 7½ miles (12km) W of Alnwick

A small village divided by the River Aln, Whittingham was involved in both the Border Wars and the Civil War, primarily because of its central position in the Vale of Whittingham. Today this tranquil village with its red pantile-roofed cottages and creeper-covered walls, could easily be mistaken for a southern English village but for the remains of its pele tower. This 14th-century tower with its 8ft-(12.4m) thick walls was restored in 1845 and converted into an almshouse.

Below Whittingham Tower a pretty path leads along the tree-lined river to a small bridge over the River Aln which links the two parts of the village. Close by on the village green is a drinking fountain topped by the statue of an old man and his dog. This is a monument to the 3rd Earl of Ravensworth.

The church of **St Bartholomew** dates from the Saxon period when Ceolwulf granted Whittingham to Lindisfarne in 737 when he entered the monastery as a monk. Only the lower sections of the Saxon tower remain, and other minor fragments. The rest of the Saxon masonry was blown up by gunpowder as part of over-zealous Victorian improvements made in 1840 when the church was enlarged.

A number of Bronze Age weapons have been discovered close to Whittingham at Thrunton Farm. They include two swords and three leaf-shaped spearheads, all in bronze and in near perfect condition. One of these weapons is known as the

Whittingham sword and is now in the Museum of Antiquities in Newcastle.

South of the village is Castle Hill, which stands above Callay. Here there is evidence of prehistoric earthworks and the scanty remains of a medieval tower that may or may not have been finished. A second 13th-century pele tower was built on the site of the current **Callay Castle**, an elegant classical mansion approached through a magnificent avenue of beech woods. A private residence, Callay Castle was built in the 18th century and contains magnificent stucco work.

WIDDRINGTON [Alnwick]

NZ2595: 7 miles (11km) NE of Morpeth

A quiet village just inland from Druridge Bay, Widdrington village was once much larger. Its modern counterpart lies one mile south-west and is built around fire clay works. Widdrington had its own castle until 1775, when it was dismantled and the stone used as building material. The site of the castle in the heart of the old village is now marked by a green mound approached through a row of limes known as the Twelve Apostles. The church of **Holy Trinity** primarily dates from the 14th century, although the north arcade is two hundred years older. In the chancel there are some sedilia, special stone seats for priests that, unusually, have been combined with a small pillar piscina or basin.

To the east of the village at Low Chibburn are the ruins of the extensive **Preceptory of St John of Jerusalem (Knights Hospitallers)**. First recorded in 1313, it was probably established to provide hospitality to pilgrims on their way to Holy Island and included a chapel. After the Dissolution of the Monasteries by Henry VII in the 16th century, the building was converted into a dower house by the Widdrington family. The current building is a rare example of a Northumbrian long house.

WOODHORN [Wansbeck]

NZ3088: 1mile (2km) NW of Newbiggin-by-the-sea

Woodhorn Colliery was a working pit from 1894 until 1981. In 1989 it was restored as a museum and the displays in the original pit buildings give a unique insight into the history of coal mining in Northumberland and what life was like for the miners and their families. The museum contains a small exhibition on Ashington football heroes including Bobby and Jackie Charlton, Jimmy Adamson and Wor' Jackie Milburn, a Woodhorn miner and North East footballing legend.

The museum is set in the **Queen Elizabeth II Country Park,** which includes a lake and small adventure playground. A railway runs from the colliery museum to the Lakeside Halt using a colliery locomotive, Black Diamond.

Woodhorn church, **St Mary's**, stands beside a little wood. It dates from Saxon times with Norman and Early English additions. Inside is a fine 13th-century effigy of Agnes de Valence, the sister-in-law of John Balliol, King of Scotland. The church is now redundant and used as a museum and cultural centre, where a regular programme of exhibitions including arts and crafts and local history is held. Close to the church are the remains of a windmill built in 1880, and probably the last windmill to be built in Northumberland.

WOOLER [Berwick upon Tweed]

NT9928: 15 miles (24km) NW of Alnwick

This small, dour market town on the edge of the Cheviot Hills still serves the surrounding moorland farms and communities of the Milfield Plain. Destroyed by fire in 1722 and again in 1862, it is a town with a turbulent past. On a key trade route between Scotland and England, it was once at the mercy of warring armies and border reivers. Not surprisingly, few buildings over a hundred years old have survived. The mound and rubble remains of the Norman castle are still visible, marked by a neo-Celtic war memorial next to St Mary's, an 18th-century church unsympathetically restored by the Victorians.

Earle Hill Museum contains a wonderful assortment of household antiquities housed in a granary – kitchen equipment, toys, christening robes, quilts, farming records and tools.

Wooler was the birthplace of the brothers George, John and Thomas **Dalziel**, who were engravers for a wide range of Victorian books and periodicals including early editions of *Punch*. Walter Scott also has links with Wooler. He stayed near here at Longleeford Farm in 1791, studying the local history and stories of the Borders.

WOOPERTON (Berwick upon Tweed)

NU0420: 6 miles (10km) SE of Wooler

In the fields around this small hamlet, on April 25th 1464, the Battle of Hedgeley was fought between the Yorkists commanded by John Neville, Lord Montague, and the Lancastrians under Sir Ralph Percy, Earl of Northumberland. The Lancastrians were defeated and Percy killed, and in the following month any final resistance by the Lancastrians was crushed at the Battle of Hexham. Ralph Percy is commemorated with a 15th-century carved pillar decorated with the Percy emblems of crescents and stars. Standing on a stone base, the cross, which is now headless, stands 10ft (3m) high. Close by are two stones known as Percy's Leap, set in a walled enclosure close to the main road. These are 8.2 metres apart and are said to mark the long leap Percy's horse took after he received his mortal wound.

WYLAM [Tynedale]

NZ1164: 2 miles (3km) NE of Prudhoe

Wylam holds a remarkable place in the history of the railways as the birthplace of three important railway pioneers: George Stephenson (1781-1848), Timothy Hackworth (1786-1850) and Nicholas Wood (1795-1865). Wylam was also where William Hedley in 1813 built his experimental steam locomotives *Puffing Billy* and *Wylam Dilly* to haul coal from Wylam colliery to the pier head at Lemington staithes. It is a story told in the little **Wylam Railway Museum** on Falcon Terrace.

George Stephenson's cottage

Just east of the village is **George Stephenson's birthplace** and the beginning of the great Stephenson dynasty. It was George who built the *Rocket*, *Locomotion* and *Number One* and his only son Robert who was responsible for the Border railway bridge at Berwick. Together with Stephenson's nephew, George Robert, they were to become great civil and locomotive engineers. The cottage built in 1750 is now in the ownership of the National Trust. It was once the home of four families, one to each room. The Stephenson family's room has been restored and is the only room open to the public. George Stephenson would have grown up surrounded by machines and coal mine workings and would have watched the horse-drawn wagons trundling along the waggonway right past the cottage.

The cottage stands alongside the Wylam and Walbottle waggonway, which is now a footpath and cycle path linking Lemington with Prudhoe and forming part of the **Tyne Riverside Country Park**. The waggonway was later used by the railway from Scotswood to Wylam which closed in 1968. The West Wylam Bridge that crosses the Tyne is also known as Hagg Bank Bridge and is part of the former railway. It was built in 1876 and was probably the first bridge in the world on which the deck was suspended from arched ribs, using the same design as the Tyne Bridge in Newcastle.

Index

A

Ad Gefrin, 8, 22, 73
Adam, Robert, 13, 20
Aethelfrith, King, 8
Agricola, 7, 63
Agricultural Shows
  Allendale Show, 15
  Shepherd's Show, Alwinton, 21
Aidan St, 9, 24, 25, 52, 64, 66, 93, 97
Alexander III of Scotland, 11, 78
Alexander, King of Scotland, 52
Alnwick Abbey, 18, 20, 57
Ancient routes and tracks
  Clennel Street, 21
  Dere street, 7, 22, 42, 59, 63, 89, 102
  Devil's Causeway, 86
  Maiden Way, 54
  Stanegate, 7, 54, 57, 81
Armstrong, Lord, 24, 90
  Cragside, 90, 91
Augustinian canons, 61, 75, 85

B

Bakethin reservoir, 71, 72
Balliol, John, 10, 11, 24, 30, 104
Bastle houses
  Akeld, 22
  Black Middens, 12, 53
  Doddington Bastle, 46
  East Woodburn, 102
  Gatehouse Bastle, 53
  High Rochester, 63
  Roses Bower, Stonehaugh, 96
  Woodhouse Bastle, 12, 67
Battles
  Bannockburn, 10 - 11, 58
  Carham, 100
  Flodden, 11, 34 - 35, 43, 47, 51, 53, 83, 100
  Haildon Hill, 11, 31
  Hamildon Hill, 68
  Hedgeley, 105
  Hexham, 46, 63, 105
  Otterburn, 11, 49, 68, 84, 97
Bede, Venerable, 8
Belford Hall, 28
Belsay Hall, 28
Benedictine Monks, 23, 93
Benedictine Nuns, 66, 74
Berwick Castle, 30
Beveridge, Lord, 97
Bewick, Thomas, 78, 85
Blagdon Hall, 96
Blenkinsopp Hall, 57
Bloodybush, 72
Bonomi, Ignatius, 27, 46, 95
Bothal Castle, 34
Brinkburn Priory, 52, 75, 76, 78
Brizlee Tower, Alnwick, 20
Bronze Age Beaker Folk, 6
Brown, Lancelot 'Capability', 13, 20, 38, 73
Bruce, Robert the, 10 - 11, 30, 58, 96
Bulter, Josephine, 46, 72
Burns, Robert, 43
Bywell Hall, 36, 37

C

Cadwallon, King, 8
Callay Castle, 104
Carmelite Order of White Friars, 20
Carter Bar, 35
Catcleugh Reservoir, 35
Cement Menagerie, Branxton, 35
Ceolwulf, King, 47, 83, 100, 103
Chain Bridge Honey Farm, 67
Charles I, 67, 89
Charlton, Bobby and Jack, 23, 104
Cheviot Hills, 4, 6, 10, 22, 46, 70, 72, 78, 105
Churches
  All Saints, Rothbury, 90
  All Saints, Ryal, 92
  All Saints, Thropton, 97
  Christ Church, Hepple, 61
  Haydon Old Church, 60
  Holy Cross, Haltwhistle, 57
  Holy Cross,Chatton, 39
  Holy Trinity Church, Cambo, 38
  Holy Trinity, Berwick upon Tweed, 30
  Holy Trinity, Embleton, 50
  Holy Trinity, Kirkburn, 84
  Holy Trinity, Matfen, 77
  Holy Trinity, Widdrington, 104
  Holy Trinity, Whitfield, 103
  St Aidan, Bamburgh, 24
  St Aidan,Throckrington, 97
  St Andrew, Bolam, 33
  St Anne, Ancroft, 22
  St Bartholomew, Kirkwhelpington, 73
  St Bartholomew, Newbiggin, 81
  St Bartholomew, Whittingham, 103
  St Bartholomew,Cresswell, 45
  St Cuthbert, Allendale, 15
  St Cuthbert, Bedlington, 26
  St Cuthbert, Bellingham, 27
  St Cuthbert, Beltingham, 29

St Cuthbert, Corsenside, 43
St Cuthbert, Elsdon, 49
St Cuthbert, Farne Island, 93
St Cuthbert, Greenhead, 54
St Cuthbert, Haydon Bridge, 60
St Cuthbert, Norham, 83
St Ebba, Beadnell, 26
St Francis of Assisi, 35
St Giles, Birtley, 31
St Giles, Chollerton, 41
St Giles, Netherwitton, 81
St Gregory the Great, Kirknewton, 72
St Helen, Longhorsley, 76
St James, Newton, 82
St James, Shilbottle, 95
St John of Beverley, St John Lee, 15
St John the Baptist, Edlington, 47
St John the Baptist, Ulgham, 98
St John's, Lowick, 76
St John, Meldon, 78
St John, Whitfield, 103
St Laurence, Warksworth, 100
St Mark, Ninebanks, 82
St Mary, Belford, 28
St Mary, Blanchland, 32
St Mary, Holystone, 66
St Mary, Holy Island, 65, 93
St Mary, Ledsbury, 75
St Mary, Longframlington, 75
St Mary, Morpeth, 80
St Mary, Ovingham, 85
St Mary, Ponteland, 86
St Mary, Stamfordham, 96
St Mary, Woodhorn, 104
St Mary & St Michael, Doddington, 46
St Mary & St Patrick, Lambley, 74
St Mary Magdalane, Whalton, 102
St Maurice, Eglingham, 47
St Maurice, Ellingham, 48
St Michael and All Angels, Alnham, 17
St Michael and All Angels, Ford, 53
St Michael and All Angels, Watchen, 98
St Michael, Alnwick, 19
St Michael, Alwinton, 21
St Michael, Felton, 52
St Michael, Howick, 68
St Michael, Ilderton, 69
St Michael, Ingram, 70
St Michael, Wark on Tyne, 99
St Mungo, Simonburn, 95
St Nicholas, Cranlington, 44
St Nicholas, West Kyloe, 76
St Oswald, nr. Wall, 98
St Paul, Branxton, 35
St Peter and Paul, Longhoughton, 76
St Peter, Chillingham, 40
St Peter, Falstone, 51
St Peter, Humshaugh, 69
St Peter, Newbrough, 81
St Philip and St James, Rock, 89
St Waleric, Alnmouth, 17
United Reformed Church, Falstone, 52
Cistercians, 10, 80
Coal industry, 14
Collingwood, Admiral, 69, 79
Comyn, John, 54, 96
Country Parks
Bedlington Country Park, 26
Bolam Lake, 33
Druridge Bay, 45
Plessey Woods Country Park, 26
Queen Elizabeth II Country Park, 104
Tyne Green Riverside Country Park, 63
Tyne Riverside Country Park, 106
Wansbeck Riverside Park, 23
Cragside, 91
Crindledikes, 25
Cromwell, Oliver, 31, 47, 67, 81
Cuthbert, St, 9, 17, 23, 43, 60, 62, 64, 65, 93

D

Dalziel, George, John and Thomas, 105
Darling, Grace, 23, 25, 38
Davison, Emily Wilding, 80
Defoe, Daniel, 4
Derwent Reservoir, 33
Derwentwater, Earls of, 45, 75
Dobson, John, 13, 15, 28, 33, 37, 50, 53 - 54, 59, 66, 69, 78 - 81
Dominicans or Black Monks, 37
Douglas, Earls of, 84
Archibald, 31, 68
Drake Stone, Harbottle, 59
Dunstanburgh Castle, 44, 77

E

Edward I, 10 - 11, 24, 30, 37, 48
Edward II, 11, 24
Edward III, 24, 31, 34, 58, 100
Edward IV, 24
Edwin, King, 8
Eglingham Hall, 47
Elfwald, King of Northumbria, 62, 99
Elizabeth I, 24, 83
Elizabethan Ramparts, Berwick, 30
Ellingham Hall, 48
English Heritage
Baracks, Holy Trinity Church, Bewick, 31
Belsay Hall, 28
Brinkburn Priory, 76
Chesters, 40
Corstopitum, Corbridge, 42
Dunstanburgh Castle, 44
Etal Castle, 50
Lindisfarne Priory, 65

Norham Castle, 83
Prudhoe Castle, 86
Warkworth Castle, 101
Etal Manor, 51

F

Fairs and Festivals
Allendale Fire Festival, 16
Alnwick Fair, 18
Ovingham Goose Fair, 85
Whalton Bale fire, 102
Flambard, Bishop, 83
Forster, Tom, 32

G

Gaunt, John of, 44
Gooch, Daniel, 26
Great Whin Sill, 5, 8, 24, 44, 93
Grey, second Earl, 68

H

Hackworth, Timothy, 105
Hadrian's Wall, 7
Birdoswald, 55
Brocolitia, 81
Chesters, 40
Heddon on the Wall, 60
Planetrees, 98
Poltross Burn, 55
Vindolanda, 7, 25
Willowford Bridge, 55
Haining Deer Farm, 97
Harbottle Castle, 58
Hareshaw Dene, 27
Heatherslaw Mill, 53
Hedley, William, 105
Henry I, 84
Henry II, 10, 24, 49, 58
Henry IV, 24, 48, 74
Henry V, 12, 48
Henry VI, 46, 63
Queen Margaret, wife, 45, 63
Henry VII, 104
Henry VIII, 10, 35, 65
Hexham Herbs, 41
Hexham to Alston turnpike, 103
High Yarrow Farm, 52
Hodgson, John, 59, 73
Holywell Dene, 94
Howick Hall, 68
Hudson, Edward, 65
Hulne Park, Alnwick, 20
Hulne Priory, Alnwick, 20

I

Iron age hill forts
Alnham, 17
Borough Law, 70
Camp Knowe, 22
Castle Hill, 6
Dod Law, 46
High Knowles, 17
Greaves Ash, 70
Harehaugh Camp, 61
Humbleton Hill, 68
Kyloe Hill, 76
Lordenshaw, 6, 91
Old Bewick, 84
Ringses, 46
Ros Castle, 21, 40
Roughton Linn, 46
The Ringses, 47
Tosson Burgh, 53
Warden, 98
Wether Hill, 70
Witchy Neuk Camp, 61
Yeavering Bell, 72, 73

J

Jacobite rebellion, 31, 33, 45, 52, 56, 75, 90
James IV of Scotland, 35, 43, 51, 53, 83, 100
Jekyll, Gertrude, 66, 102
John, King of England, 52, 59, 78, 79, 80, 90

K

Kielder Forest, 5, 53, 70, 72
Kielder Water, 71, 88
King David of Scotland, 10
Kirkley Hall, 86
Kyloe Hills, 76

L

Lancaster, Thomas Earl of, 44
Langley Castle, 74
Lead-Mining Industry, 13, 15 - 16, 41
Blackett's Level, 15
Langley smelt mills, 74
Sopwith, Thomas, 16, 39
Lighthouses
Blyth, 33
Coquet Island, 23, 101
Longstone Island, 93
St Mary's, 94
Lilburn Tower, 45, 69
Lindisfarne Gospels, 9, 65
Linhope Spout, 70
Lutyens, Edwin, 31, 65, 96, 102

M

Malcolm Cranmore, King of Scotland, 20, 84
Malcolm II of Scotland, 100
Marlish Farm, 60
Medieval crosses
- Blanchland, 32
- Bywell, 37
- Comyn's Cross, 96
- Malcolm's Cross, Alnwick, 20
- Ulgham, 97

Meldon Park, 78
Mesolithic period, 6
Milburn, Jackie, 23, 104
Mitford Castle, 78
Moot Hall, Hexham, 62
Motehills, Elsdon, 48
Museums and Heritage Centres
- Borough Museum and Art Gallery, Berwick Barracks, 30, 31
- Brigantium Centre, 89
- Kings Own Scottish Borders Museum, Berwick, 31
- The Museum of Island Life, 64
- Woodhorn Church, 104

N

National Trust
- Aidan's Dunes, 92
- Allenbanks, 29
- Cherryburn, 78
- Cragside, 91
- Druridge Bay, 45
- Lady's Well, Holystone, 66
- Limekilns, Beadnell, 26
- Low Newton, 77
- Ros Castle, 40
- St Cuthbert's Cave, Belford Moor, 28
- Wallington Hall, 38

Nature Reserves
- Amble Dunes, 23
- Druridge Bay, 45
- Far Skeer, 92
- Harbottle Crags, 59
- Holystone Burn, 67
- Low Hauxley, 23

Neolithic period, 6
Netherwitton Hall, 81
Newminster Abbey, 80
Newton Hall, 82
North Pennines Area of Outstanding Natural Beauty (AONB), 5
Northumberland National Park
- Information Centre, Ingram, 70
- Information Point, Falstone, 51

Nunnykirk Hall, 81
Nunwick Hall, 95

O

Ogle Castle, 84
Oswald St, King of Northumbria, 9, 24, 64, 98
Otterburn Mill, 85
Otterburn Training Area, 88

P

Paine, James, 28, 37
Paulinus St, 8, 22, 24, 66
Pele towers, 12
- Ancroft Church, 22
- Callay, 104
- Cocklaw Tower, 41
- Crawley Tower, 86
- Cresswell Tower, 45
- Duddo Tower, 47
- East Kyloe Tower, 77
- Elsdon Tower, 49
- Farne Island, 93
- Haltwhistle, 57
- Harbttle, 59
- Hepple tower, 61
- Horsely Tower, 76
- Newton Hall Tower, 82
- Ninebanks Tower, 82
- Pele tower, Ford, 53
- Preston Tower, 48
- Shilbottle, 94
- Staward pele, 29
- Thropton Tower, 97
- Tosson Tower, 53
- Vicar's pele tower, Alnham, 16
- Vicar's pele, Corbridge, 42
- Vicar's pele, Ponteland, 86
- Whittingham, 103

Pennine Way, 96
Percy family, 10
- Alnwick, 18
- Harry (Hotspur), 68, 84, 101
- Prudhoe castle, 86
- Ralph, 105

Preceptory of St John of Jerusalem (Knights Hospitallers), 104
Prehistoric standing stones
- Battle Stone, 73
- Duddo, 47
- Five Kings, 67
- Goatstones, 95
- Great Swinburne, 56
- Stob stone, Matfen, 77
- Three Kings, 35
- Threestoneburn, 69
- Warrior Stone, Ingoe, 69

Premonstratensian Canons or White Monks, 20, 32, 36
Puiset Bishop Hugh de, 83

R

Railways
- Allendale Branch Railway, 74
- Alnwick-Coldstream railway, 47, 72
- Alston-Haltwhistle branch line, 57, 74
- Border Counties Railway, 27, 41, 48, 72, 87
- Heathershaw Light Railway, 53
- Newcastle, Carlisle railway, 55, 74
- Scotswood to Wylam railway, 106
- South Tynedale Railway, 74
- Stockton and Darlington railway, 26
- Tweedmouth to Kelso branch line, 83
- Wannie and Rothbury railway, 38
- Wansbeck railway, 87
- Wylam and Walbottle waggonway, 106
- York, Newcastle and Berwick railway, 83

Ratcheugh Crag, 76
Ridsdale Ironworks, 88
Rock Hall YHA, 89
Roman remains
- Bremenium, 7, 49, 63, 66
- Brocolitia, 81
- Chesters, 40
- Chew Green, 7, 22
- Corstopitum, Corbridge, 42
- Habitancum, fort, 102
- Robin of Risingham, 102
- Roman fort, Powburn, 86
- Vindolanda, 25

Ros Castle, 40
RSPB reserves
- Newton Pool, 77
- Coquet Island, 23

S

Salvin, Anthony, 19, 69, 75, 89, 95, 101
Saxon crosses
- Rothbury, 9, 90
- Warden, 99

Scott, Sir Walter, 11, 21, 55, 82, 105
Seaton Deleval Hall, 94
Shaw, Norman, 91
Simonside Hills, 91
Sites of Special Scientific Interest (SSSI)
- Bamburgh Dunes, 25

Smeaton, John, 43, 57
South Tyne Trail, 74
Stephenson
- Mabel, mother of George, 85
- Robert, 30, 105

Swinburne, John of Capheaton, 72, 95

T

Tarset Castle, 54
Telford, Thomas, 79
Thirwall Castle, 97
Trevelyan, Charles, 38
Turner, JW, 44, 76
Turnpike trusts, 13
Twizell Bridge, 43

U

Umfraville family, 49
- Prudhoe castle, 86
- Robert, 58, 66

Union Chain Bridge, 67

V

Vanbrugh, John, 31, 79, 94

W

Waggonways, 14
Wallace, William, 11, 74
Wallington Hall, 37
Walltown Quarry, 54
Wark (on Tyne) Castle, 99
Wark Forest, 95
Waterloo Stones, 82
Wesley, John, 17
Whittingham sword, 104
Wilfrid St, 9, 61, 65
William the Conqueror, 9
William the Lyon, King of Scotland, 10, 57, 78, 87, 100
Wood, Nicholas, 105

Also of interest from: SIGMA Leisure

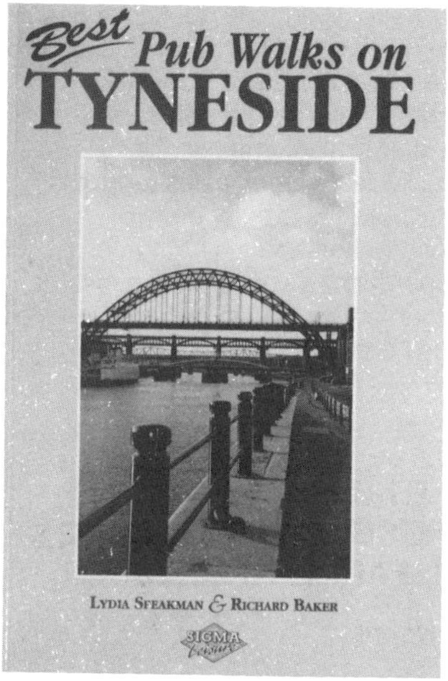

BEST PUB WALKS ON TYNESIDE

Lydia Speakman & Richard Baker

With this book, co-written by Lydia Speakman – the author of "Towns & Villages of Northumberland" – Tyneside, which is already an area noted for its quality beer and pubs, is also becoming renowned for its fine walking.

£6.95

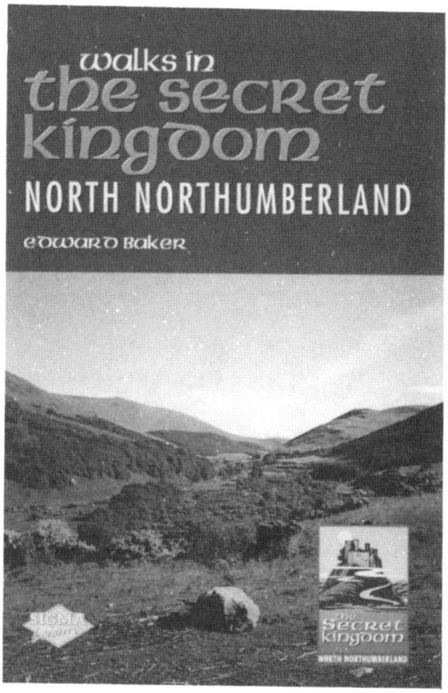

WALKS IN THE SECRET KINGDOM: North Northumberland

Edward Baker

Explore the varied landscape and unique character of North Northumberland with this book of easy-to-follow, flexible routes, written by an experienced Northumbrian author. "This book will appeal to all ages, from the long-distance walk hunter, to the family group just wanting to fill in a few hours... and at the same time get some worthwhile exercise." BORDER TELEGRAPH

£6.95

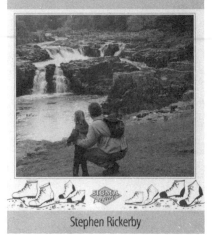

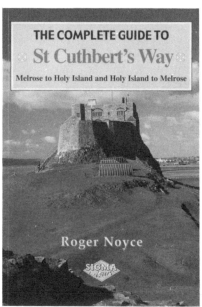